The JOY of Believing

A PRACTICAL GUIDE TO THE CATHOLIC FAITH

MOST REV. WILLIAM E. LORI,
ARCHBISHOP OF BALTIMORE

theWORD
among us®
press

19 18 17 16 15   2 3 4 5 6

ISBN: 978-1-59325-271-7
eISBN: 978-1-59325-466-7

The chapters in this book were originally published as a series of articles in *Columbia* magazine published by the Knights of Columbus.

Unless otherwise noted, Scripture texts in this work are taken from the New American Bible, revised edition © 2010, 1991, 1986, 1970 Confraternity of Christian Doctrine, Washington, D.C., and are used by permission of the copyright owner. All rights reserved. No part of the New American Bible may be reproduced in any form without permission in writing from the copyright owner.

Excerpts from the English translation of the *Compendium of the Catechism of the Catholic Church*, copyright © 2005, Libreria Editrice Vaticana. All rights reserved. The exclusive licensee in the United States is the United States Conference of Catholic Bishops, Washington, DC, and all requests for United States uses of the *Compendium of the Catechism of the Catholic Church* should be directed to the United States Conference of Catholic Bishops.

Excerpts from the English translation of the *Catechism of the Catholic Church* for use in the United States of America, copyright © 1994, United States Catholic Conference, Inc. – Libreria Editrice Vaticana. Used with permission.

Cover design: David Crosson
Photo credit: Thinkstock Images

Made and printed in the United States of America

Library of Congress Control Number: 2015932442

Contents

Foreword

By Carl A. Anderson
Supreme Knight, Knights of Columbus

In promulgating the *Catechism of the Catholic Church* in 1992, St. John Paul II stated, "For me . . . Vatican II has always been, and especially during these years of my Pontificate, the constant reference point of my every pastoral action" (*Fidei Depositum*, 1). At that time, the pope recognized that a deepening of our understanding of the faith was foundational to the mission of renewal for the Church called for by the Council. He saw that the Church was challenged to continue to transmit the faith, but to do so "in a new way in order to respond to the questions of our age" (3). To do this was essential if Christians were to fulfill "their mission of proclaiming the faith and calling people to the Gospel life" (4).

Twenty-five years later, today's Christians find themselves surrounded by a multiplicity of challenges: secularism, hedonism, multiculturalism, relativism, religious conflict, and even a new emerging hostility to religion itself. Taken together, these cultural dynamics pose new questions about the meaning of "belief," "faith," and the Christian "way" of life—questions that find their answer in the *Catechism of the Catholic Church*. But how to make the nearly seven hundred pages of the *Catechism* accessible to every individual, as St. John Paul II had asked?

This was the task that Archbishop William Lori set for himself as Supreme Chaplain of the Knights of Columbus month after month in the pages of our magazine, *Columbia*. His very personal and insightful presentations have been appreciated by hundreds of thousands of brother knights. It is now with pleasure that we make his reflections available to readers beyond the members of the Knights of Columbus and their families.

Pope Francis has written his first apostolic exhortation on joy. There is spiritual genius in his choice of the title, *The Joy of the Gospel,* and, indeed, in the fundamental presentation of his document. It comes at a time when too many see the Christian way of life as opposed to joy, or at least as opposed to the pursuit of happiness. Pope Francis urges us to recall that the authentic Christian life must be lived in joy. Perhaps too often we have forgotten this truth. But the Gospels are clear on the relationship between joy and a life lived in response to God's love. Christ himself gives this explanation: "I have told you this so that my joy may be in you and your joy may be complete" (John 15:11).

Joy as essential to the Christian life has also been a consistent theme of Pope Benedict XVI. For example, in commenting on St. Luke's account of the Annunciation, he observed that the angel's use of the word "Rejoice!" (cf. Luke 1:28) communicates to us a great lesson: "The first word of the New Testament is an invitation to joy" (Homily, December 18, 2005).

Joy is at the center of the new evangelization. Today the power of individual witness cannot be underestimated. A joyful witness of evangelization—of authentic love of God and neighbor—can move hearts in a way that words alone cannot.

This was the powerful attraction of Blessed Teresa of Calcutta and of St. John Paul II. It is also why so many throughout the world are drawn to the message of Pope Francis. The authenticity of joy in living out the Gospel attracts people. And the authenticity of our joy as Christians should do the same. As Pope Francis pointed out in *The Joy of the Gospel,* such joy prompts a person to share it with others. Like love, joy is truly itself when it is shared with others, introducing other people to the love that inspires such joy (1–5).

Through his death and resurrection, the Lord has opened up to us the possibility of "sharing in an eternal life of love" (Hans Urs von Balthasar, *The Moment of Christian Witness,* p. 57). What other response can we appropriately have to such "Good News" than to "Rejoice"! But to do so in a way that is worthy of a true disciple requires that we know better the content of our faith, the guidelines of our moral life, and the beauty of our worship and prayer. We are grateful to be accompanied on this path by the profound and deeply pastoral reflections contained in *The Joy of Believing*.

Carl A. Anderson has served as the Supreme Knight of the Knights of Columbus since 2000. He has also been a member of several Vatican commissions and committees for the United States Conference of Catholic Bishops. He is the author of several books, including the New York Times *bestseller* A Civilization of Love: What Every Catholic Can Do to Transform the World.

Introduction

After two of Jesus' future disciples heard John the Baptist say, "Behold, the Lamb of God," they began trailing him. Jesus turned around and saw them. Then he asked them a most important question: "What are you looking for?" (John 1:35-37). Here Jesus wasn't offering to provide them with information or directions. He was asking about the inmost desire of their hearts.

Jesus addresses the same question to us. Amid the ups and downs of life, amid our triumphs, tragedies, and daily routines, what is it that our hearts persistently desire? There's something in us we can't quite shake that urges us to look deeper than our most basic needs. That something is our "religious sense" (Pope Francis, *Evangelii Gaudium* [The Joy of the Gospel], 72); it is an inbuilt desire for God. Without his love, our lives make no sense (see St. John Paul II, *Redemptor Hominis* [The Redeemer of Man], 10). And the love for which we are made is God's infinite love. As the lyrics of an old song put it, we want to be loved "not for just an hour, not for just a day, but always."

Faith is the door that unlocks for us this relationship of love for which we long. It is a gift given us by the Holy Spirit in Baptism, but like all God's gifts, faith has to be developed. We might think of developing our faith in these terms: As a man and woman fall in love, they begin to believe in one another and to trust one another. They also want to know as much about each other as they can. They become interested in one another's family background, in each other's core values and convictions, in one another's likes and dislikes. In other words, knowledge and love go hand in hand.

There is no substitute for a deep and personal encounter with the Person of Christ or, as a poem attributed to Jesuit Fr. Pedro Arupe put it, for "falling in Love in a quite absolute, final way." But our falling in love entails believing and trusting in Jesus Christ, who leads us to the Father in the power of the Holy Spirit. As Jesus' love for us takes root in our hearts and our love for Jesus begins to grow, it is then that we become disciples—those who want to learn from Jesus because we want to follow him. The more his love overtakes our hearts, the more our minds are opened to his truth, even those truths that are difficult to understand or those truths that may challenge the way we think or relate to others. Yet when we know and love the Lord, believing is not the path to drudgery but to joy, the joy the Holy Spirit gives us when our whole being—mind, body, and spirit—is being transformed by God's wisdom and love.

It is in this spirit that I offer this book, which, in effect, is a summary of a summary of what the Church believes and teaches. It all began with a meeting hosted by Supreme Knight Carl A. Anderson for the chaplains of the Knights of Columbus. The subject was how chaplains throughout the order could assist their brother Knights in coming to know and love their faith more fully. As the meeting proceeded, the chaplains asked if I would use my monthly column in *Columbia* to offer brief explanations of the faith that could be used at council meetings. It was further suggested that I base my articles on the *Compendium of the Catechism of the Catholic Church*, which was relatively new. So for the next three years or so, I never had any trouble figuring out what the subject of my monthly column in *Columbia* would be!

Now that this series has been completed, I would like to offer it not only to my brother Knights, but also to a wider audience as a reliable summary of the faith, for individual reading or for use in groups. While it can serve as a resource for understanding the Church's teaching, even more do I hope that it will help many see how the faith relates to their lives—especially their desire for God's love—and especially in the context of prayer and study groups. For that reason, questions for personal reflection and group discussion have been added to the conclusion of each chapter. Also featured at the beginning of each chapter is a relevant Scripture passage.

No explanation of the faith, in and of itself, leads to joy. Joy is a fruit of the Holy Spirit. My hope and prayer is that this book might help individuals and groups open their hearts to the Lord, who is the source of all love, truth, joy, and peace. God bless you and keep you always in His love.

Most Reverend William E. Lori
Archbishop of Baltimore
January 17, 2015

1. "Athirst Is My Soul"

Man's Capacity for God and God's Plan for Man

Compendium: 1–10
Scripture Passage: Psalm 63:1-8

One Sunday evening I happened to catch a weekly news show on TV, and one particular segment caught my attention. The anchor was interviewing a gentleman who owned what is arguably the largest and most technologically advanced sailboat in the world. When the reporter asked him about its price tag, the man demurred; all he would reveal was that the boat cost more than a hundred million and less than three hundred million. Burrowing in, the reporter proceeded to ask him about his owning such a stunning luxury, not to mention his other boats, cars, and homes. In spite of himself, this poised and accomplished man mentioned the plight of the poor. But he left unanswered the question of whether so many possessions had brought him happiness and fulfillment.

Of course, possessions alone—even world-class possessions—do not bring happiness. It is not that possessions are bad. The problem is that they are not good enough to satisfy the human spirit. The Catholic Church tells us why: "God himself, in creating man in his own image, has written upon his heart the desire to see him. Even if this desire is often ignored, God never ceases to draw man to himself because only in God will he find and live the fullness of truth and happiness for which he never stops searching" (*Compendium of the Catechism of the Catholic Church*, 2).

This is a perennial truth that confounds modern culture yet also gives hope to millions of saints and sinners the world over. Christopher Hitchens' book *God Is Not Great* is a good example of how this truth annoys many of those around us. With energetic vitriol but little attention to accuracy, Hitchens, an avowed atheist, sets out to debunk the central religious claims of Judaism, Christianity, and Islam. Enlightened and resistant rationality, he argues, should replace religious faith, and the sooner the better! Judging from his rhetoric, I would guess that Hitchens (and others like him) are frustrated that we believers are still around and are still a force to be reckoned with.

In our age of unbelief, when Catholicism is often ridiculed by late-night comedians and lambasted in the press, hundreds of thousands of people each year still seek to be baptized and become members of the Church. But make no mistake: Hitchens speaks for many. His book, despite its fatal flaws, spent many weeks on *The New York Times* best-seller list. Experience also teaches that even believers can fall into the trap of living as if God does not exist.

Nothing Else but God Will Do

Yet atheism of all sorts faces a difficult climb. The steepest part of this climb is the inbuilt longing for God that is part of every human being's "standard operating equipment." All of us ask basic questions about the meaning of life such as "Who am I?" and "Why do I exist?" We reflect on our desire to love and to be loved. We also wonder why life can be a struggle and why there is illness, heartbreak, and so much evil in the world. We think about death and what happens to us after death. Reason can help answer our most profound questions but does not go the whole way. In reality, these basic questions indicate an intense longing for God deep within us; nothing else but God will do.

In the fifth century, St. Augustine wrote a book called the *Confessions*. In it he tells the story of his conversion to Christianity, a story that continues to inspire us today. Among its most quoted lines are these: "You are great, O Lord, and greatly to be praised. . . . You have made us for yourself, and our heart is restless until it rests in you" (Book I, Chapter 1; *Catechism of the Catholic Church* [CCC], 30).

Faith and Reason

The human spirit is made for love—ultimately, for God's infinite love. People search for this love in ways that are ennobling but also in ways that are destructive. We can be distracted in our search; even other believers can sometimes lead us astray. Nevertheless, we cannot escape the desire for God's love. Atheism simply cannot deny this universal and relentless search of the human heart for the love of God.

Our search is not futile. On the contrary, God revealed himself to us both through the created world in all its wonder and through his plan of redemption. We are awestruck when we gaze into the starlit sky or look upon a beautiful landscape. The harmony, order, beauty, and purposefulness of creation signal to our reason the existence of an intelligent Creator. And while reason alone can determine that such a Supreme Being must exist, nonetheless, "there is another order of knowledge, which man cannot possibly arrive at by his own powers, the order of divine Revelation" (CCC, 50). In a word, we really cannot know God until our power of reason is enlightened by faith.

Faith is what enables us to see that God not only created a marvelous universe, but that he also freely and lovingly planned for us to come to know and love him intimately as he revealed himself and drew near to us in human history. What a crucial message "in a world where the name of God is sometimes associated with vengeance or even a duty of hatred and violence!" (Pope Benedict XVI, *Deus Caritas Est* [God Is Love], 1).

God's Plan

In many ways, God's plan to save us and draw us to himself is what "the joy of believing" is about. It is about the intrinsic link between God's love and human love (*Deus Caritas Est*, 1). The *Compendium* sums up God's plan in one breathtaking sentence. It speaks of a plan "of sheer goodness" in which God "freely created man to make him share in his own blessed life. In the fullness of time, God the Father sent his Son as the Redeemer and Savior of mankind, fallen into sin, thus calling all into his Church and, through the work of the Holy Spirit, making them adopted children and heirs of his eternal happiness" (1). This is God's plan: to go in search of us despite our sinfulness and our substitution of possessions and false loves for his true and everlasting love.

For Personal Reflection and Group Discussion

1. In what ways have you experienced God revealing himself to you? How have you responded?

2. In what do you find your happiness and fulfillment? What possessions or false loves might you substitute for God's love?

3. In what areas of your life have you fallen into the trap of living as if God does not exist or as if you are ignoring him? What might have contributed to this attitude?

_____

_____

_____

_____

_____

4. What might you do to concretely express your faith in God and your desire to put him at the center of your life?

_____

_____

_____

_____

_____

5. What relationship or interaction between faith and reason do you recognize and experience in your own life?

_____

_____

_____

_____

_____

2. God's Way of Coming to Us

Scripture, Tradition, and the Magisterium

Compendium: 11–24
Scripture Passage: 1 Timothy 2:4

Recently I was traveling by train from New York to Washington, D.C. A passenger boarded at Newark and sat next to me. After he observed my Roman collar, we started discussing religion. We agreed on the importance of achieving greater understanding among the great world religions. It was during the time of Pope Benedict XVI's pontificate, and so we also discussed the Holy Father's sustained efforts to reach out to the Islamic and Jewish communities in perilous times. I tried very hard to convince my fellow traveler, a non-practicing Catholic, that one religion simply is not as good as another—that the Christian religion is the true faith and that Catholicism is the fullest and truest expression of the Christian faith. I may have succeeded if the train had been going to Florida and we'd had more time to discuss the matter.

The key point that I was trying to make is that the Christian religion is not, in the first instance, our approach to God, but rather God's way of coming to meet us. God revealed himself to us. He spoke and acted in human history. Although human reason can conclude that God certainly does exist, we can truly know and love God only because he has chosen to reveal himself to us. So the Christian religion is not merely a matter of personal conjecture and preference; it is based on God's revelation. The glossary of the *Catechism of the Catholic Church* describes "revelation" as "God's communication of himself, by which he makes known the mystery of his divine plan" to save the world. God manifests himself in history by words and deeds that go together to convey his truth and love.

The high point of revelation occurred when God the Father sent his only Son, the second Person of the Trinity, into the world. In the Incarnation, God's only Son assumed our human nature by the power of the Holy Spirit, becoming like us "in every way, yet without sin" (Hebrews 4:15). Humanity became the means by which God would most fully reveal and communicate himself to us. Or as the Second Vatican Council's *Sacrosanctum Concilium* (Constitution on the Sacred Liturgy) put it, "[Christ's] humanity, united with the person of the Word, was the instrument of our salvation" (5). The liturgy itself drives home this same truth when, addressing God the Father, it says, "You came to the aid of mortal beings with your divinity and even fashioned for us a remedy out of mortality itself" (Preface III of the Sundays in Ordinary Time). God has revealed himself in ways entirely suited to our humanity so that we might share in his divinity in an eternal relationship of love.

The Bible: Unified and Coherent

Revelation—that is, God's self-communication—comes to us in two thoroughly interrelated ways. The first way is through the Scriptures. The Bible is not one book but a collection of books accepted by the Church as the authentic, inspired record of God's revelation of himself to humanity and his will to bring about the salvation of all. It is divided between the Old Testament and the New Testament. The Old Testament contains forty-six books "which record the history of salvation from creation through the old alliance or covenant with Israel, in preparation for the appearance of Christ as Savior of the world" (CCC, Glossary). The New Testament contains the twenty-seven books of the Bible written during the time of the apostles. These books include the four Gospels; the Acts of the Apostles; the letters of Sts. Paul, James, Peter, John, and Jude; and the Book of Revelation. They record and communicate what Christ, the incarnate Son of God, said and did to save us. They tell us how he established the new and eternal covenant by dying on the cross and rising from the dead.

Although there are two major divisions in the Bible, there is a remarkable unity and coherence in the Scriptures as it relates to us God's plan of redemption and shows the path to reconciliation between God and man. (This unity is demonstrated by the Liturgy of the Word at Sunday Mass; try to notice how the Old Testament reading and the Gospel reading fit together.)

Tradition

The second way in which God's revelation reaches us is Tradition. Tradition, in this context, means much more than merely old customs. Rather, it has to do with handing on and transmitting the living message of the gospel in and through the Church. The apostles shared the Father's ultimate revelation of his life and love in his son Jesus Christ by their inspired preaching, by their example (especially martyrdom), and by the institutions they established. As the Second Vatican Council's *Dei Verbum* (Dogmatic Constitution on Divine Revelation) explains, the apostles shared what they had received from the lips of Christ, from his way of life and his works, and from what they had learned through the prompting of the Holy Spirit (7). The Scriptures and the preaching of the apostles are "conserved and handed on" as the living heritage of the Church's faith, known as the "deposit of faith." Thus, we receive the word of God, "the entire content of Revelation as contained in the Holy Bible and proclaimed by the Church" (CCC, Glossary). "Both Sacred Tradition and Sacred Scripture make up a single deposit of the word of God which is entrusted to the Church" (*Dei Verbum*, 10).

At the Service of God's Word

The Lord made yet another provision to ensure that his life-giving word would reach us untainted by error. He provided for the Magisterium, the living teaching office of the Church. The Magisterium alone has the task of providing an authentic interpretation of the word of God, whether in the form of Scripture or tradition. Its authority is exercised in the name of Christ (*Dei Verbum*, 10; CCC, 85). The task of authentically interpreting the word of God continues to be exercised by the Holy Father and the bishops throughout the world in union with him. The Magisterium fulfills this task by being the servant of God's word. Obedient to God's command and guided by the Spirit, the Magisterium listens to the word of God with reverence, guards it with dedication, and explains it faithfully (CCC, 86). Although many people today think of the Magisterium as being out of touch or authoritarian, it is, in fact, a great gift that guides us toward a right understanding of what God himself has revealed.

By studying the faith, we are better positioned to accept the Holy Spirit's invitation to understand and accept the revelation of God in Jesus Christ. Revelation is God's way of making it possible for us to respond to him—truly knowing and loving him in a way that goes beyond our natural powers of understanding. For that, we are eternally grateful!

For Personal Reflection and Group Discussion

1. Do you find it hard to accept that the Christian religion is the true faith and not merely a matter of personal conjecture and preference? Why or why not?

2. What is the core of God's revelation to humanity? How would you explain God's revelation of himself in the Christian faith to an atheist or a person of another religion?

_____

_____

_____

_____

3. Why does the Catholic Church consider Scripture the inspired word of God?

_____

_____

_____

_____

_____

4. Give a few concrete examples of how obeying God's word has changed you or something in your life.

_____

_____

_____

_____

_____

5. How have the teachings of the Church deepened and strengthened your relationship with the Lord? With the universal Church?
With your local parish?

_____

_____

_____

_____

_____

3. Our Response to God

FAITH IS A GIFT TO BOTH RECEIVE AND SHARE

Compendium: 25–35
Scripture: Luke 1:26-38

When ordering dinner in a good restaurant, we sometimes ask the waiter, "What do you recommend?" Chances are, we are inclined to follow the waiter's suggestion. Or when checking in for a flight, we might ask if the plane is running on time. If the ticket agent looks at the computer and replies, "Yes, it is," we tend to accept that as true. My point is not to comment on food or travel but to say that in daily life, we take many things on faith—on the word of another—especially if that person is deemed to be "in the know."

The Obedience of Faith

Faith in God is both similar to and profoundly different from ordinary human faith. At a minimum, divine faith means we accept as true what God has revealed. In doing this, we acknowledge God's goodness and authority. After all, he is not just reliably "in the know" but all-knowing, all-powerful, and all-loving. But faith in God is much deeper than the faith we accord to other human beings. The faith we put in God is a response to God who has revealed himself to us. The *Compendium* teaches that "we respond to God with the obedience of faith, which means the full surrender of ourselves to God and the acceptance of his truth insofar as it is guaranteed by the One who is Truth itself" (25). This is much more than finding out a bit of useful information and taking it to be true. Rather, when we respond in faith to God, we are bound in loving obedience to him and to all that he has revealed. Faith is God's gift to us by which we are enabled to acknowledge and remain in his presence—and to follow his commandments. Thus, we speak of "the obedience of faith" (Romans 16:26).

There are many examples of men and women of faith to inspire us. The preeminent example of faith, of course, is the Blessed Virgin Mary. Her whole life can be summed up by the words "May it be done to me according to your word" (Luke 1:38). In our lifetime, we have had two saints, St. John Paul II and Blessed Mother Teresa of Calcutta, who certainly exemplified the intrepid and persistent spirit of faith-filled obedience to the mission that God had in mind.

The Gift of Faith in a Skeptical Age

Faith is both a gift from God and a fully human response necessary for salvation. Perhaps you have heard the expression that faith is an "infused virtue." The word "infused" simply means that God freely gives us faith as a supernatural gift to enlighten our mind and will; it is to be distinguished from an "acquired virtue" that, through the workings of God's grace, we attain by practice or repetition of good deeds. In Christ and through the Holy Spirit, the Father pours the gift of faith into us. Faith is "the realization of what is hoped for," and such hope "does not disappoint, because the love of God has been poured out into our hearts through the holy Spirit that has been given to us" (Hebrews 11:1; Romans 5:5).

But infusion is not osmosis! The seeds of faith planted at Baptism must grow through our fully graced and fully human assent to God and to all he has revealed. Our response must include listening to the word of God as it comes to us through the Church and therefore growing in knowledge and love of what God has revealed to us through the Scriptures and Tradition. For this reason, we can see the vital importance of evangelization (proclaiming and witnessing to Christ) and catechesis (systematic instruction in the truths of the faith). As our faith—and thus our personal adherence to Christ—grows, we begin in some way to live here and now the blessed life that we will experience fully in heaven.

In a skeptical age, it is not always easy to be a person of faith. Today there is a newly militant atheism underfoot, which claims that faith, far from shedding the light of truth on God and the human condition, is a dangerous, prescientific distortion and the root of serious problems such as terrorism. Attacks on faith, of course, are nothing new. As Catholics, we should face these challenges confidently. We see faith as an ally, not an enemy, of reason. Although faith is above reason, it enlightens reason in two important ways: by helping us to grasp the supernatural truths that faith teaches and by clarifying what reason can know on its own. We are reminded that "there can never be a contradiction between faith and science because both originate in God. It is God himself who gives to us the light both of reason and of faith" (*Compendium*, 29).

One Lord, One Baptism

Faith, of course, is intensely personal, but it is not one's private possession. The *Catechism* teaches that faith is both personal and "ecclesial," that is, "of the Church." Enlightened by faith, we embrace the Church's faith. Therefore, when we profess our faith, we say, "I believe" (*Credo*) in company with fellow members of the Church. "It is in fact the Church that believes: and thus by the grace of the Holy Spirit precedes, engenders, and nourishes the faith of each Christian" (*Compendium*, 30). We receive the gift of faith through the Church, and faith is nourished in and through the community of believes.

From childhood, most of us have been taught formulas of faith. These are accurate, time-honored expressions of what the Church believes and teaches, developed under the influence of the Holy Spirit. The most common summaries of the faith are the Nicene Creed and the Apostles' Creed. As the *Catechism* reminds us, we believe not in formulas themselves but in the divine realities they express and that faith allows us to touch (CCC, 170). It is important for us to know and understand these formulas as a sure guide in our lives of faith. After all, we are a Church with over a billion members and two millennia of history. We are sinners and saints made up of people of every nation, tongue, and culture. Yet we confess "one Lord, one faith, one baptism," to the glory of God and the salvation of our souls (Ephesians 4:5). We should never let a day go by without thanking God for our faith and asking him to increase it.

For Personal Reflection and Group Discussion

1. Were there specific moments in your life when you realized that your faith in God had increased? Did something happen to precipitate this realization?

2. Why do you think we often struggle with obedience to God's will and commandments? How might it help to ask the Lord for an increase in faith?

3. What sort of things (for example, a practice or devotion) can you do, or do you already do, to help your faith grow?

_____

_____

_____

_____

_____

4. In what ways is your faith nourished by the Church and the community of believers? How does the faith of others bolster your own?

_____

_____

_____

_____

_____

5. What does it mean to you that you share your faith with billions of believers, past and present? How can that truth strengthen you in your daily walk with the Lord?

_____

_____

_____

_____

_____

4. Our Faith's Foundation

DISCOVERING AND KNOWING THE ONE TRUE GOD

Compendium: 36–43
Scripture Passage: Deuteronomy 6:4

I believe in one God, the Father almighty, maker of heaven and earth, of all things visible and invisible." This is the first line of the Nicene Creed, which we recite every Sunday at Mass. It affirms one's personal belief, joined to the Church's communal belief, in the existence of God. The most fundamental affirmation of our faith, it is key to all that the Church believes and teaches. It is also fundamental to how we look at our own lives, the society in which we live, and the world itself.

If God did not exist, both human life and creation would lose their transcendent meaning. The world and those who dwell in it could no longer be seen as reflecting the goodness of an all-powerful God who is above and beyond the created universe. In addition, we would not have a destiny beyond our present experience.

Refuting the "New Atheism"

In the previous chapter, I noted that a resurgence of atheism is underway. Its advocates do not make new arguments to discredit belief in God; rather, they take advantage of an increasingly secular culture to rehash old and shaky arguments. In my view, there are two good ways to counter neoatheism. The first is to live our faith with integrity and love. The second is to deepen our awareness of why the Church remains confident in the power of reason, even when unaided by the light of faith, to arrive at the truth that God exists.

We can know the existence of God as we reflect on the beauty and order of creation and ponder how our world and the universe itself came to be. We can detect his existence in the continual urgings of our conscience to do good and avoid evil, and in the restlessness of our hearts for a fulfillment that nothing in this world can provide. As Pope Francis in his first encyclical *Lumen Fidei* (The Light of Faith) pointed out, 'There is an urgent need . . . to see once again that faith is a light, for once the flame of faith dies out, all other lights begin to dim. The light of faith is unique, since it is capable of illuminating *every aspect* of human existence" (4). And Pope Benedict XVI convincingly argued in his encyclical *Spe Salvi* (On Christian Hope) that human reason is truly human when it "looks beyond itself." Only then does reason perceive the dangers of god-lessness to human dignity (23).

"I Am Who I Am"

Most of us, I would venture to say, know God first and foremost because he has revealed himself to us and has given us the gift of faith. Enlightened by faith, we more readily see the reasonableness of maintaining God's existence. Faith does not destroy reason but enables it to look more competently beyond itself. Faith also allows us to hold fast to God as the foundation of our existence and to assent to all he has revealed.

God has revealed himself in creation and in the history of salvation. He also revealed himself to his chosen people as the only true and living God: "Hear, O Israel! The LORD is our God, the LORD alone" (Deuteronomy 6:4). Again and again, the prophets confirmed that there is only one true and living God and reproached the people whenever they fell into idolatry. Jesus also confirmed that there is only one God.

Not only did God reveal to the Israelites that he is the one and only God, but he also revealed his name to them. First he was known as "the God of Abraham, the God of Isaac, and the God of Jacob," indicating how he guided and protected the people of Israel. God also revealed his mysterious name to Moses in the episode of the burning bush—"I am who I am" (YHWH)—reflecting that God is the very fullness of being and indeed remains utterly steadfast, gracious, and forgiving in his relationship with the people of Israel (Exodus 3:14, 15). Jesus also applied the mysterious name "I AM" to himself to indicate his divine Sonship (John 8:28).

In revealing his name to the people of Israel, God did not merely provide information about himself. He revealed "the riches contained in the ineffable mystery of his being" (*Compendium*, 40). God's name indicates that he has always existed and will always exist. It tells us that he exists above and beyond the universe and history. It also tells us that he created the world and all that is in it. All created things borrow existence from God; God alone is the fullness of being. Unseen, he is completely spiritual. He is "transcendent, omnipotent, eternal, personal, and perfect" (40).

God Is Love

God's name also shows his closeness to his people and his determination to protect and forgive them. As we read the books of the Old Testament, we see a growing awareness, thanks to the Holy Spirit, of how God's transcendent greatness fits together with his nearness to his people.

The *Compendium* sums up God's attributes by saying, "He is truth and love" (40). Scripture affirms not only that God is truthful (he can never deceive nor be deceived), but that he is the origin of all that is true, wise, and good. "God, who alone made heaven and earth, can alone impart true knowledge of every created thing in relation to himself" (CCC, 216). God's word is utterly trustworthy when he reveals himself to us, especially through his Son Jesus who came "to testify to the truth" (John 18:37).

God also revealed himself as love. He loved the people of Israel with a passionate spousal love, a love that was fully revealed and fulfilled in Christ. That is why St. Paul in Ephesians speaks of Christ's nuptial love for the Church: "Husbands, love your wives, even as Christ loved the church and handed himself over for her" (Ephesians

5:25). Ultimately, in Christ, God was revealed not merely as the doer of loving deeds but as love itself: "God is love" (1 John 4:8, 16).

Reflecting on God's majesty and greatness will deepen our faith. It will also inspire in us a spirit of trust and thanksgiving, especially in times of difficulty. The stronger our faith in God, the more willing we are to defend human life and its God-given dignity.

For Personal Reflection and Group Discussion

1. Do you simply recite the Profession of Faith without thinking, or do you recognize it as a meaningful affirmation of your belief in the existence of God and his Lordship over you? Try taking each line of the Nicene Creed this week and praying about each line and what it means to you.

_____

_____

_____

_____

_____

2. In what ways does human reason support and/or undermine your faith in God? Explain your response.

_____

_____

_____

_____

_____

3. What does the revelation of God's name "I am who I am" (Exodus 3:14) indicate to you about God himself?

_____

_____

_____

_____

_____

4. God has revealed himself to humankind as love. Describe some examples of how you personally perceive and experience God's love.

_____

_____

_____

_____

_____

5. Recall how your faith in God and your knowledge of his love sustained you in the midst of a particularly difficult or trying time in your life.

_____

_____

_____

_____

_____

5. Father, Son, and Holy Spirit

THE ONE GOD HAS REVEALED HIMSELF AS A TRINITY OF PERSONS

Compendium: 44–49
Scripture Passage: Matthew 3:13-17

Many years ago, I attended a parish anniversary that happened to fall on Trinity Sunday. The homilist spent about a minute on the Trinity, the central mystery of the Christian faith. In effect, he dispensed with it as an impenetrable mystery beyond anyone's power of understanding. He then launched into a string of charming stories drawn from the history of the parish.

Everyone enjoyed his homily, but, in fact, it shortchanged the congregation, which consisted of Christians baptized in the name of the Triune God. It also did not do full justice to the parish as part of the Church, described by the Second Vatican Council as a people "made one by the unity of the Father and the Son and the Holy Spirit" (*Lumen Gentium* [Dogmatic Constitution on the Church], 4; *Compendium*, 153). Indeed, the Trinity is a mystery that sheds light on every aspect of our faith and our lives, as we shall see with greater clarity as we progress through the chapters of this book.

In the previous chapter, I tried to show how our reason can lead us to discover the existence of God and even some of his attributes. While it is true that hints of God's Trinitarian love are found in creation and in the Old Testament, the mystery of the Trinity can be known only because the one God has revealed himself as a trinity of Persons. This mystery was revealed when God's Son assumed our humanity and entered into human history.

The Trinity is the most sublime and central mystery of our faith. Far from being a mere puzzle or an irrational assertion, the mystery of the Trinity both exceeds and elevates the powers of reason. As a result of God's self-revelation in and through Jesus Christ, we can come to a much clearer understanding of who God is—without, of course, attaining full knowledge of his infinite majesty and glory.

Jesus Reveals the Father and the Holy Spirit

God the Father was revealed through Christ's life, teachings, and saving deeds. Jesus taught us that God the Father is the beneficent Creator. Recall, for instance, his words about the birds of the air and the lilies of the field (Matthew 6:26-28). Even more so, Jesus showed us his relationship with the Father, which we see when Jesus becomes absorbed in prayer. We hear it in Jesus' teaching when he tells us that he came from the Father and was returning to him (John 14). We share in Jesus' relationship with God the Father through his loving obedience to the Father's saving will, expressed by the love Jesus embraced on the cross.

Jesus also revealed the Holy Spirit. From Scripture we learn that Jesus was conceived by the power of the Holy Spirit and that the Spirit hovered over him at his baptism and at the Transfiguration. After his death and resurrection, Jesus breathed the Holy Spirit upon the apostles, empowering them to forgive sins. Finally, the Holy Spirit descended upon the apostles and the Virgin Mary at Pentecost.

Reflecting on these episodes and teachings from the Gospels, the Church definitively teaches that the Father eternally generates the Son and that the Son is eternally generated by the Father. The living, eternal bond of love between the Father and Son is the Person of the Holy Spirit (*Compendium*, 48).

This helps us understand what is meant when the Church expresses its Trinitarian faith: "one God in three Persons." Notice that Father, Son, and Holy Spirit are not merely three names for God or merely three ways in which the one God might appear. Nor should we think of the Trinity as three gods cobbled together in a corporate partnership. There really is only one God, yet with three distinct Persons (the Father is not the Son and the Son is not the

Father, etc.). The three Persons of the Trinity possess completely and coequally the divine nature. They are three identifiable Persons, each fully God in a manner that is distinct yet related to the others (*United States Catholic Catechism for Adults*, 52).

A Love beyond All Telling

Because the Trinity is so great a mystery, we may be tempted to side with the aforementioned homilist who decided to gloss over this teaching in favor of sharing personal anecdotes. However, to do so would miss the most beautiful teaching of the New Testament: God is love. The complete self-giving of the three Persons of the Trinity, each to the others, reveals to us a love beyond all telling, a love that the Trinity has lavished upon us in creation and redemption, and a love we are called to share through Baptism. It is a passionate but not a self-seeking love, a love that is beautifully described in Pope Benedict XVI's first encyclical, *Deus Caritas Est*. This is the love that illuminates everything we believe in and hope for as Catholic Christians. It is the mystery of a communion of love that gives joy and meaning to our lives as we seek union with God and unity with one another.

I am reminded of a particularly challenging homily I once had to give. One Trinity Sunday as I arrived at church, I learned to my complete surprise that I was scheduled to celebrate the children's Mass. It was immediately clear that my prepared homily would just not do, but as the moment approached, I had no clue how to present this sublime mystery in a vocabulary the children would understand.

I was praying to the Holy Spirit for help when I blurted out, "Who knows how to make the Sign of the Cross?" Everyone did. I then asked, "Is there one God or three?" A bright little girl answered, "Oh, Bishop, there's only one God, but he has three Persons."

"Out of the mouths of babes," I thought as I pressed on. "Well, who are the three Persons?" I asked. The same little girl said, "Father, Son, and Holy Spirit" and added, "Bishop, everyone knows that!"

For Personal Reflection and Group Discussion

1. What do we know of God through Jesus' revelation of him to us?

_____

_____

_____

_____

_____

2. How would you describe or explain the Trinity? What is the best description you've ever read or heard?

_____

_____

_____

_____

_____

3. How has the Holy Spirit been revealed to us by Jesus? Give a few specific examples from the Gospels.

_____

_____

_____

_____

4. In what concrete ways do you see the Holy Spirit at work in your life?

_____

_____

_____

_____

_____

5. How do you relate to each Person of the Trinity in your prayer and in your daily life?

_____

_____

_____

_____

_____

6. Creationism versus Evolution

*By Believing That God Created the Universe,
We Do Not Reject the Value of Science*

Compendium: 50–65
Scripture Passage: Genesis 1:1-25

Few things have caused more heated discussion in our country than the question of whether evolution or creationism should be taught in the public schools. Sometimes I am tempted to think that the debate has hardly progressed since the famous Scopes trial in 1925. William Jennings Bryan and Clarence Darrow argued over whether John Scopes, a Tennessee high school teacher, should be permitted to teach his students ideas borrowed from Charles Darwin's book *The Origin of Species*. Today in many quarters, the public debate is still creationism versus evolution.

Sections 50–65 of the *Compendium* are a good guide for understanding why we call God "Creator" and remain open to what science can legitimately teach us about the world around us. These sections are a reflection on these words of the Nicene Creed: "I believe in one God, the Father almighty, maker of heaven and earth."

Almighty and Eternal God

From all eternity, God the Father begets his only Son, through whom he created and redeemed the world. Although creation was an act of the Trinity, the work of creation is particularly ascribed to God the Father (*Compendium*, 52). This suggests that the mighty work of creation is the result of God's fatherly, providential love. He created the universe out of love and continues to sustain it in love.

Infinite in being, God is also infinite in his power. He did not have to create the world but, in his wisdom, freely chose to do so (*Compendium*, 54). The *Compendium* teaches that "his omnipotence is universal, mysterious, and shows itself in the creation of the world out of nothing and humanity out of love" (50). The greatest display of God's fatherly and almighty power is his mercy, which is revealed in the Incarnation of his Son and in the paschal mystery (Jesus' death and resurrection). Power and love do not merely coexist in God; they coincide. All created things—"visible and invisible," the world, together with the angels—manifest God's goodness, truth, and beauty (53; 59–61).

The Bible: Theology, Not Science

The Apostles' Creed speaks of God as the "creator of heaven and earth." Let us consider the ordinary way that we use the words "creator" and "creation." We often speak of innovative composers, designers, and writers as "creators" and their works as "creations." Of course, their works are not entirely original but always depend on what has come before. Only God is Creator in the strict sense. He created the universe "out of nothing" (*Compendium* 54: cf. 2 Maccabees 7:28). Regardless of how old it is, the universe did not always exist. It came into being thanks to God's creative hand.

The biblical accounts of creation in chapters 1 and 2 of Genesis are not meant to be scientific accounts. Rather, they have a theological purpose. They show us that creation is the foundation of all God's plans. This is why creation is especially dear to him. It is how he communicates his merciful love for us, which culminates in Christ.

The world's order and goodness, its beauty and wonder, are not ends in themselves. They are meant to open us to the goodness and beauty of the inner life and love of the Trinity in which we are called to share. Thus, "the world is not the result of any necessity, nor of blind fate, nor of chance" (*Compendium*, 54). Rather, the world exists for God's glory. Creation reflects God's providential care for us. Through life's joys and sorrows, God leads us toward our destiny to share his life and love forever with all the redeemed (55–56).

Good and Evil

In Scripture we read that when God looked upon what he had made, he saw that it was good. If that is so, how did evil come about? The reality of evil is often cited as an argument against a good and all-powerful God. We all struggle with the evil we experience in ourselves and in the world. In a sound-bite culture, the mystery of evil does not admit easy answers. We might say, along with the *Compendium*, that the answer to evil is the whole of God's plan to reveal himself in creation and history and to redeem the world. The key to understanding evil is, ironically enough, God's love. In his love for us, God did not choose to create a perfectly self-contained and completely predetermined world. Instead, he created a world in which we are able to go beyond ourselves in freedom and love and encounter the living God.

God did not create evil or will its existence, but he does permit it. In his omnipotent love, he brings forth good from evil. The ultimate example of this is Jesus' death on the cross. We are called to alleviate human suffering and conquer evil with God's love, which has been poured out into our hearts by the Holy Spirit (Romans 5:5) .

Points of Debate

As we have seen, both the Bible and the Creed treat creation as the foundation of God's plan of redemption, not simply as a matter of science. This should help us understand the debate between creationists and evolutionists. The Church preserves and protects what we must believe regarding God as Creator and his purpose in creating all things. The Church does not require us to interpret the creation accounts in Genesis "literally." We are to draw from them their original intent, especially when viewed in the context of the whole story of creation and redemption as it unfolds in the Bible. On the other hand, the Church's teaching authority guards against all-inclusive explanations for creation that go beyond the limits of scientific method and exclude God's all-important role.

The Church is especially clear in rejecting theories of evolution in which the human person is reduced simply to a product of natural forces. The Church rightly insists that each human soul requires God's creative intervention. Otherwise, the teaching authority of the Church wisely refrains from making judgments about various theories of evolution—as long as such theorizing does not overreach to exclude God as author and designer of the universe and as the creator of each human person.

For Personal Reflection and Group Discussion

1. Discuss your understanding of God as Creator and the theory of scientific evolution. Do you think they are mutually exclusive?

_____

_____

_____

_____

_____

2 In what ways do you see God's creative power continuously at work in the world today?

_____

_____

_____

_____

_____

3. How do you explain and deal with evil and chaos in the world around you?

_____

_____

_____

_____

_____

4. What is the relationship between God's work of creation and his plan of redemption?

_____

_____

_____

_____

_____

5. Describe some concrete examples of how you have seen God bring good out of evil.

_____

_____

_____

_____

_____

7. The Dignity of Man

ONLY HUMANS ARE CREATED WITH THE CAPACITY TO KNOW, LOVE, AND SERVE GOD

Compendium: 66–70
Scripture Passage: Genesis 1:26-31

As the proud owner of two golden retrievers who go by the names of "Barnes" and "Noble," I readily took a call from a fellow dog lover during a call-in radio show I used to host. But the caller's question got me into trouble. She wanted to know if her dog would go to heaven. I made it clear that the beatific vision is for human beings and angels, not our cherished pets. She was pretty unhappy when she heard my reply, and so were other callers. It was tough to read my "fan mail" that week. Not long after that, the radio station gave my airtime to a call-in sports show.

I thought of my ill-starred radio career when reflecting on something our culture increasingly forgets—namely, that human beings are created "in the image of God" and possess a dignity unmatched by the rest of creation (Genesis 1:27). Today some people paradoxically champion animal rights yet support abortion, which is the taking of innocent human life. Others, in an effort to protect the environment, assert by some of the policies they advocate that human beings are not really the pinnacle of God's creation. In fact, one environmentalist argued that trees are more important than humans because without trees, humans wouldn't be able to breathe!

Why Did God Make Us?

It stands to reason that we must protect the environment. In addition, successive popes and the Church's social teaching have taught that we human beings must respect and protect creation. At the same time, we also must take care not to lose our God-given place in it. While all creation reflects God's wisdom and love, only man was created "in the image of God" (Genesis 1:27). In order to see what this phrase means, let's go back to what we studied about the Trinity. We were made to reflect the creative, life-giving, and utterly generous love that characterizes the relationship between the Father, Son, and Holy Spirit. Our human capacity for truth and our ability to be loved and to love—however limited by nature and wounded by sin they may be—reflect something of God's inner life.

The Church also teaches that man is "the only creature on earth which God willed for its itself" (Vatican II, *Gaudium et Spes* [Pastoral Constitution on the Church in the Modern World], 24). This means that God willed us into being for no reason other than his love for us. Simply put, God did not need us but he wanted us to share in his infinite truth, beauty, goodness, and love. This is the key to our human dignity. Since God values us for our own sake, so too should we value others for their own sake. In other words, we should not treat people like objects. Among other things, this means rejecting lustful temptations to treat people as objects of desire and refusing to treat defenseless persons as mere instruments for research purposes, such as with the case of embryonic stem-cell research.

Since we live in a world where human dignity is constantly threatened, we need to reflect even more seriously on the question "Why did God make us?" The *Baltimore Catechism* states that we were made to know, love, and serve God in this life and to be happy with him in the next. This teaching, so often forgotten in today's world, has ancient roots. In the last part of the second century, St. Irenaeus of Lyons wrote, "The glory of God is man fully alive; moreover man's life is the vision of God." He went on to say, "If God's revelation through creation has already obtained life for all beings that dwell on earth, how much more will the Word's manifestation of the Father obtain life to those who see God?" (St. Irenaeus, cited in CCC, 294).

These words are timeless, and they say something very important for us today. When Irenaeus states, "The glory of God is man fully alive," he is telling us that God delights in us, in our humanity and in the many gifts he has given us (see Isaiah 62:3). These gifts include our bodies, our intelligence, our freedom, and our ability to love. Truly, "We are all the work of [his] hand" (64:7). Our uniqueness is not merely genetic. We are a unity of body and soul—a material body given us by our parents and a spiritual soul that God directly creates (*Compendium*, 69–70).

St. John Paul II often stated that each person is an "unrepeatable reality" (see, for example, *Redemptor Hominis*, 14). What is more, the human race shares a common origin in God the Father, "from whom every family in heaven and on earth is named" (Ephesians 3:15). Accordingly, human dignity and rights are given to us, not by any human authority or government, but by God. We are thus responsible for building a just and tranquil society that respects human life and dignity.

Called to Greatness

But let us make sure we understand two things that St. Irenaeus is *not* saying. First, when he states that "the glory of God is man fully alive," he is not reducing God's glory merely to the human level. In other words, he is not justifying certain trends in theology and secular culture that make us choose between God's greatness, which is far above us (his transcendence), and God's closeness to us and to our humanity (his imminence). God glories in us while remaining the God of "glorious majesty" (Eucharistic Prayer I). Second, Irenaeus is not endorsing the contemporary view that a life with only casual reference to our Creator is good enough.

Irenaeus' message becomes clear when we look at what he says next: "Man's life is the vision of God." Here he is teaching that our human dignity lies in the fact that we are the only creatures who can freely "know, love, and serve God." When we do this, we do not lose our identity, intelligence, talents, or freedom. Our humanity is not compromised but is instead fulfilled by our friendship with

God. Our search for truth and love here on earth is aided, not hindered, by the light of God's truth and love dwelling in our minds and hearts. Indeed, our being known and loved by God, and our knowing and loving him in return, is what constitutes the fulfillment of all our desires. To be "fully alive" means embracing, right in the heart of earthly existence, where we have come from and where we are going.

The mere fact that we are called to eternal friendship with God means we possess a dignity beyond compare. We are called to live and work in the world and yet we are not to be of the world (John 17:14-15). We, living on earth, are called to a greatness that goes beyond earthly existence.

For Personal Reflection and Group Discussion

1. "God created mankind in his image" (Genesis 1:27). What attributes and characteristics of God are reflected in our human nature?

   _____

   _____

   _____

   _____

   _____

2. Cite some example of how contemporary society threatens human dignity. Has your own dignity ever been impinged upon? If so, how did you respond?

   _____

   _____

   _____

   _____

   _____

3. Have you ever experienced God "delighting" in you? If this is a difficult concept for you to embrace, ask God to help you experience a sense of the pleasure he takes in you for the unique being that you are.

_____

_____

_____

_____

_____

4. In what concrete ways do you value and express your regard for the dignity of others, recognizing each person an "unrepeatable reality" (St. John Paul II)?

_____

_____

_____

_____

_____

5. In what particular way(s) is it challenging and difficult for you to be in the world yet not of the world (John 17:14-15)?

_____

_____

_____

_____

_____

8. "Male and Female He Created Them"

THE COMMUNION OF LOVE BETWEEN A HUSBAND AND
WIFE FINDS ITS ULTIMATE SOURCE IN GOD

Compendium: 71–72
Scripture Passage: Genesis 2:18-24

Previous chapters have reviewed the teaching of the *Compendium* on the creation of the world and the human family. I hope those reflections provided not only solid teaching about creation, but also helped to engender a sense of wonder and awe toward God the Creator. This chapter will build on what was already said about the creation of the human person in the image of God. Let us turn our attention to a seemingly simple statement found in the opening pages of Scripture: "God created mankind in his image; / in the image of God he created them; / male and female he created them" (Genesis 1:27).

Being created "male and female" has something to do with being made in God's image. One's sexual identity is not merely a matter of psychology, physiology, or appearance. It is not a "style" of being human, nor a feeling prompted by sexual attraction or inclination. On the contrary, "maleness" and "femaleness" are part of God's creative design and go to the depths of one's very being. The *Catechism* teaches this truth: "Man and woman have been *created*, which is to say, *willed* by God: on the one hand, in perfect equality as human persons; on the other, in their respective beings as man and woman. 'Being man' or 'being woman' is a reality which is good and willed by God: man and woman possess an inalienable dignity which comes to them immediately from God their Creator" (369).

Equal and Complementary

Let's be clear: The human person was made in God's image but "in no way is God in man's image" (CCC, 370). Sexual differences do not exist in God, who is "pure spirit" (370). However, the differences among the three Persons of the one God help us understand that "being man" and "being woman" are two equal and complementary ways of being human. In other words, God's plan calls for man and woman to help and support each other and thus form a communion or bond of love. According to the *Catechism*, "God created man and woman *together* and willed each *for* the other" (371).

In his design for creation, God united man and woman and ordained that they bring new life into the world through their love for one another. He commanded them, "Be fertile and multiply" (Genesis 1:28). In forming a communion of love, the couple cooperates with God in the procreation of new human life. This truth, etched into the design of creation, is at the heart of the Church's teaching against contraception expressed in Blessed Paul VI's 1968 encyclical *Humanae Vitae* (Of Human Life).

Now we are prepared to return to the question of how "maleness" and "femaleness" reflect the inner life of the Trinity. How does our being created male and female have something to do with our being made in God's image? A quote from St. John Paul II's 1988 apostolic letter *Mulieris Dignitatem* (On the Dignity and Vocation of Women) will help us see this connection:

> The fact that man "created as man and woman" in the image of God means not only that each of them individually is like God, as a rational and free being. It also means that man and woman, created as a "unity of the two" in their common humanity, are called to live in a communion of love, and in this way to mirror in the world the communion of love that is in God, through which the Three Persons love each other in the intimate mystery of the one divine life. The Father, Son and Holy Spirit, one God through the unity of the divinity, exist as persons

through the inscrutable divine relationship. Only in this way can we understand the truth that God in himself is love (cf. 1 John 4:16). (7)

Infinite, Immense, and Never-Ending

Reflecting on that passage, we see the depth and beauty of the communion of love that is at the heart of the vocation of marriage. St. John Paul II makes clear that the love of husband and wife is an image of the love of the divine Persons. This can be seen in several ways. For instance, we may observe that the love of the divine Persons is characterized by absolute self-gift and reception of the other. In other words, their love is not something they give, as with a product or commodity; rather, they give themselves, their very being. The love they share is not something that can be traded or calculated—and the gift of love is not payment for having received love. When love is truly a gift of self, there is no calculation, just the full, free gift of one's being. This love that the Father and the Son give and receive is the Holy Spirit, who can be called their gift, their bond, even their communion. The Holy Spirit is not being exchanged between the Father and the Son; he is not traded, calculated, or measured. Like the Father and the Son, he is holy, eternal, infinite, immense, and never-ending.

If human love is to imitate divine love, it, too, should not be calculated, measured, or exchanged as a commodity. In a creaturely and therefore limited way, this love should be holy, moving toward the eternal.

Furthermore, in the Father and Son's love for one another, there is perfect unity in difference, which is inherently and infinitely fruitful. Each of the divine Persons is fully divine, but in a way the other is not. Similarly, as St. John Paul II pointed out, male and female are two distinct ways of being fully human. God ordained their union in married love and mutual self-donation to welcome new life as a fruit and sign of their love for one another.

This truth—a truth that many find difficult to understand or accept—is in fact worthy not only of our assent but also of our active attention. It is at the heart of the Catholic Church's efforts to support family life and to defend the institution of marriage for the common good of society, for the sake of the Church, and for the salvation of the human family.

For Personal Reflection and Group Discussion

1. What is the origin and basis of human sexual identity—"maleness" and "femaleness"?

2. Discuss the significance of the differences between and complementarity of "being man" and "being woman." What are some concrete examples?

3. In what ways is contemporary society denying or devaluing the differences between men and women?

4. How is the love of husband and wife an image of the love of the divine Persons?

_____

_____

_____

_____

_____

5. If you are married, how might you deepen the "communion of love" with your spouse?

_____

_____

_____

_____

_____

9. The Fall

*Scripture and Tradition Shed Light on
the Origin and Mystery of Evil*

Compendium: 73–78
Scripture Passage: Genesis 3:14-15

How many times have you heard this question: "Why is there sin and evil in the world?" Although the question of evil is difficult, we must address it realistically in the light of faith. Conversely, any attempt to explain the Christian faith that downplays the reality of sin and evil will fall short.

Of course, serious questions about suffering and evil are nothing new. Many of the psalms ask why God-fearing people often suffer while the lawless seem to have it easy. The question is posed most sharply in the Book of Job. Again and again, Job is tempted to denounce the God who has allowed him to experience evil and suffering in so many forms. Job does not curse God, but neither can he offer a definitive answer to why he is suffering. As we shall see in future chapters, it is Jesus Christ who offers the real answer to human suffering, especially by his passion, death, and resurrection. For now, however, the question that concerns us is this: where did sin and evil come from in the first place?

Angels and Demons

Many today would dismiss an explanation of the existence of evil based on an ancient biblical story. Ruling out biblical wisdom in favor of science, they would prefer to explain sin "as merely a developmental flaw, a psychological weakness, a mistake, or the necessary consequence of an inadequate social structure" (CCC, 387). To be sure, these factors help explain much about human behavior—but they do not answer the question of where sin and evil originate. As the

Compendium puts it, "This reality of sin can be understood clearly only in the light of divine revelation and above all in the light of Christ the Savior of all" (73).

Revelation helps us see that evil and sin are more than defects in humanity or creation. Clearly affirming the goodness of God's creation, Scripture and Sacred Tradition teach that sin and evil first began with the rejection of God by Satan and other fallen angels. Angels are pure spirits who were created to contemplate God's glory and serve as his messengers (*Compendium*, 60). The angels have also been endowed with freedom and thus are moral beings. Some of them made an irrevocable decision to reject God and his kingdom. In doing so, they chose to live in their own godless "space," their own hell.

To be sure, we believe in the existence of angels as a matter of faith. Science can neither prove nor disprove their presence. Nonetheless, Satan's rejection of God helps us understand the magnitude of the battle between good and evil. In describing the victory of Christ over sin and death, the Church's liturgy says, "Death and life have contended in that combat stupendous: / the Prince of life, who died, reigns immortal" (Easter Sunday Sequence, *Victimae Paschali Laudes* [Praise the Paschal Victim]). This hymn helps us see redemption not merely as our own private escape into paradise, but as a struggle of cosmic proportions.

The third chapter of the Book of Genesis teaches that human beings are not immune from the fallen angels' original rejection of God. Human beings, like angels, were created in freedom. When that freedom emerged in an original couple at the dawn of human history, it was well attuned to God and to all that was good in creation. Adam and Eve exercised their freedom in harmony with God and experienced his friendship. The description of the verdant garden in Genesis depicts not only the goodness of creation, but also a sense of communion between God and man and between man and the rest of creation. Yet in his cleverness, Satan gradually seduced our first parents to doubt God's friendship and to replace it with something else.

The Original Sin

In creating the universe and beings that share in his own freedom, God takes the risk of love. He has endowed both angels and human beings with freedom because he willed into creation a world where love is possible. Love means the lover freely chooses the beloved and vice versa. It also means that the lover can love someone or something else in place of the beloved. Adam and Eve, who were our representatives at the daybreak of human history, chose to replicate the sin of the fallen angels. They chose to be "like God" on their own terms—that is to say, the masters of their own lives and destiny apart from God. This was the original sin.

Scripture teaches that our first parents, in rejecting God, lost something very precious for those who would come after them: "the original grace of holiness and justice" (*Compendium, 75*). Although human dignity and goodness were not lost completely, the natural harmony and friendship between the human family and God were radically disrupted. All human beings—save the Blessed Virgin Mary, by a singular grace—are born with original sin, that is, "the state of deprivation of original holiness and justice" (76).

In a classic TV episode of the 1970s sitcom *All in the Family*, Edith tries to persuade her daughter, Gloria, and her son-in-law to have their baby baptized. Unhelpful as usual, Archie, Edith's husband, asks what sin a four-month-old child could have committed. Among the many things Archie does not understand is that original sin is not a personal act but rather an inherent part of the human condition. This inherited sin speaks to the shared human tendency to reject God and to choose what is evil. Even those who do not accept the Church's teaching about original sin can see the results of it in the human inclination to sin and in the enigma of death.

In the face of both angelic and human rejection of his love, God, the consummate lover, did not choose to withdraw his love but rather to lavish it all the more. "God did not abandon man to the power of death" (*Compendium*, 78). Instead, we find in Genesis

3:15 an initial proclamation of the gospel: "that evil would be conquered and that man would be lifted up from his fall" (78). This was the initial announcement of the coming of the Redeemer, "born of a woman" (Galatians 4:4). So great was this Redeemer that on Holy Saturday, the Church sings of the sin of Adam and Eve as a "happy fault."

For Personal Reflection and Group Discussion

1. Where did evil and sin originate?

_____

_____

_____

_____

_____

2. How does recognizing Satan's rejection of God help you grasp the magnitude of the battle between good and evil?

_____

_____

_____

_____

_____

3. What "risk of love" did God take with his creation? What did the human family lose by Adam and Eve's replication of Satan's rejection of God?

_____

_____

_____

_____

_____

4. Discuss your understanding of what "original sin" means. How do you see it in the world? In your own life?

_____

_____

_____

_____

_____

5. Why is Genesis 3:15 called the "first gospel"? What does it foreshadow and give a hint of?

_____

_____

_____

_____

_____

10. Jesus Christ, the Only Son of God

TRULY GOD AND TRULY MAN, JESUS CHRIST STANDS AT THE CENTER OF HUMAN HISTORY

Compendium: 79–97

Scripture Passage: Galatians 4:4-5

First and foremost, the annual celebration of the Advent and Christmas seasons intensifies the Church's constant proclamation of the Good News for the entire human family: Jesus, the eternal Son of the Father, was born of the Virgin Mary in the power of the Holy Spirit for our redemption and the redemption of the world. The proclamation of the name of Christ and his saving deeds is the heart of the gospel.

But who is Jesus Christ? We remember Jesus' question: "Who do people say that the Son of Man is?" (Matthew 16:13). After various opinions are offered, it is Peter who confesses the astounding truth: "You are the Messiah, the Son of the living God" (16:16). On this confession the entire life and mission of the Church has been built. Our faith in Christ should instill in us a desire to share the Good News with all those we meet—"to reveal in the Person of Christ the entire design of God and to put humanity in communion with him" (*Compendium*, 80).

What's in a Name?

The angel of God told Mary and Joseph to name the child "Jesus"—which means "God saves"—"because he will save his people from their sins" (Matthew 1:21; Luke 1:31). Jesus' name is itself a proclamation of his unique identity and saving mission as seen from the perspective of our need for salvation; in no other name can we find salvation (Acts 4:12). That is why we are never to take Jesus' name in vain.

Jesus is also called the "Christ." This is not a family name but rather a Greek term meaning the "anointed one" or "Messiah." Jesus is the long-awaited Savior sent from the Father and anointed with the Holy Spirit (Luke 3:21-22). Through Baptism we become members of the Church and heirs to all that the Lord did to save us, in obedience to his Father's will, by his life, death, and resurrection.

Jesus has a unique and perfect relationship with the Father. While we are adopted sons and daughters of the Father in Christ, only Jesus is God's Son from all eternity, the second Person of the Trinity. Both Jesus' baptism in the Jordan by John the Baptist and his Transfiguration on Mount Tabor were marked by the overshadowing Spirit and the voice of the Father: "This is my beloved Son, with whom I am well pleased" (Matthew 3:17; 17:5).

Another very important title of Jesus is "Lord," referring to Jesus' "divine sovereignty," which he demonstrated by his miracles, his control over the forces of nature, and his forgiveness of sins (*Compendium*, 84). St. Paul teaches, "No one can say, 'Jesus is Lord,' except by the holy Spirit" (1 Corinthians 12:3), and includes in his letter to the Philippians an early confession of faith: "Jesus Christ is Lord, / to the glory of God the Father" (2:11). Just as the Church's liturgy constantly addresses Jesus as "Lord," we should never let a day go by without reverently addressing Christ as did the apostle Thomas: "My Lord and my God!" (John 20:28).

Fully God, Fully Man

Why did God the Father send his Son into the world? Was there no other way to save us? Theologians have long discussed that question, but the fact remains: although Jesus was God's Son from all eternity, at a point in time some two thousand years ago, he assumed our human nature and entered history. This happened because God wanted to draw near to us, reconcile us to his love, and enable us to share his life.

Jesus is "true God and true man"—of one substance, "consubstantial" with the Father—and at the same time, truly our brother.

This central truth of our faith was authoritatively summarized and taught by the Council of Chalcedon in AD 451. It proclaimed that Jesus is a divine Person, the second Person of the Holy Trinity, with two natures, divine and human. This does not mean that Jesus is "half God" and "half man," but rather fully God and fully man. As man, he revealed the Father to us and, at the same time, revealed us to ourselves—who we are and what we should become (*Gaudium et Spes*, 22). As God, he has made us partakers in the divine nature, in the life and love he shares with his Father from all eternity.

Jesus' two natures, without becoming confused, work together. The *Compendium* states, "In the humanity of Jesus all things—his miracles, his suffering, and his death—must be attributed to his divine Person which acts by means of his assumed human nature" (89). That is why when Jesus speaks and acts in the Gospels, a wisdom, power, and love emerge that amazes and even baffles his followers and his enemies alike.

The Incarnation was real. The Son of God truly did assume "a body animated by a rational human soul" (*Compendium*, 90). As the Second Vatican Council teaches, "He worked with human hands, He thought with a human mind" (*Gaudium et Spes,* 22). In doing so, Jesus learned many things the way we do—by experience. But as God, he had an "intimate and immediate knowledge of God his Father" (*Compendium*, 90). Jesus was aware of the plan of God his Father, which he had come to fulfill. He also knew the inmost thoughts of others.

Moreover, Jesus possessed both a human and a divine will. We all know how easy it is for our wills to go awry, to know what we should do but to do something else instead. As we struggle with our fallen nature, here is a beautiful truth for us to reflect on: as the Son of God made man, Jesus willed in a human way all that the Trinity had decided upon to bring about our salvation. The human will of Christ was fully conformed to the Father's saving love. In his will we find the pattern for the obedience that should be ours as baptized sons and daughters of the Father. What is more, we have access to

Christ's obedient love through the Mass and the sacraments. Jesus' obedience serves to heal our disobedience and its effects.

And not only did Jesus humanly know and follow what he learned from his heavenly Father, but with his human heart, he also knows and loves us. For that reason, the Sacred Heart of Jesus symbolizes the boundless love of the Trinity for us.

Perhaps this is a good place to end. But it is also the beginning—the inexhaustible foundation of our life in Christ.

For Personal Reflection and Group Discussion

1. What does the name "Jesus" mean to you personally? In what concrete ways has Jesus "saved" you? How can reverencing Jesus' name and using this name to speak to him help you when you pray?

2. The title "Lord" refers to Jesus' divine sovereignty. Do you have difficulty submitting any areas of your life to Jesus' Lordship? What might prevent you from doing so?

3. Ponder and discuss the significance of Jesus' Incarnation—that is, the fact that he took on human flesh to redeem us. How would you explain the Incarnation to someone who did not believe in Jesus?

_____

_____

_____

_____

_____

4. What might you do to renew your appreciation of the wonder of Christ's Incarnation? How might you actively express your gratitude for it?

_____

_____

_____

_____

_____

5. Have you ever shared Christ and the gospel message with others? Can you think of instances when you missed an opportunity to share the good news? If so, what prevented you?

_____

_____

_____

_____

_____

11. Born to Save Us

BORN OF THE VIRGIN MARY, JESUS BRINGS NEW LIFE TO THE WORLD

Compendium: 98–105
Scripture Passage: Ephesians 1:3-14

As the New Year begins, many people make resolutions that are soon forgotten. The Church always encourages good resolutions at the beginning of the year but also brings us to the true "new beginning" that came about when Jesus was born of Mary. The Word of God, the only Son of the Father, has come into the world to make all things new (John 1: 18; Revelation 21:5). The newness of Jesus and of the life he came to give us can be glimpsed in Christ's birth and his "hidden" years at Nazareth.

"No Other Name"

When we speak about the "newness" of Jesus, this does not mean that he was simply a very interesting personality or someone with a fresh perspective. Rather, Christ is utterly unique as Lord and Savior. In accordance with God's mysterious plan for the salvation of the world, the eternal Son of the Father was "incarnate by the Holy Spirit and born of the Virgin" (Eucharistic Prayer IV).

While there have been many important religious figures and philosophers throughout history, none will ever equal or replace Jesus. Care must be taken lest even well-intentioned efforts at interfaith dialogue end up relativizing Jesus—that is, seeing him as a tremendously important religious figure but not the one and only Savior. However, our faith resoundingly attests that "there is no other name" by which we can be saved (Acts 4:12, RSV). All who are saved, including those who seek God with a sincere heart, are saved only by the love of Jesus Christ. Thus, official Church documents such as the declaration *Dominus Iesus*, issued by the Congregation for the Doctrine of the Faith in 2000, insist on what is called the "unicity" and "universality" of the Lord Jesus, the Savior (3). He is the only Savior of the entire human race.

In the Apostles' Creed, we profess that Jesus "was conceived by the power of the Holy Spirit" and "born of the Virgin Mary." In effect, we proclaim that Christ "is the Son of the heavenly Father according to his divine nature and the Son of Mary according to his human nature" (*Compendium*, 98). Often, especially during the Christmas season, the liturgy invokes Christ as "Son of God and Son of Mary." That does not mean that Jesus is two persons cobbled into one. Rather, as the *Compendium* puts it, Jesus is "truly the Son of God in both natures [divine and human] since there is in him only one Person, who is divine" (98). Of course, no other religious figure makes or can make that claim.

In both the liturgy and in private devotions, we lovingly speak of Mary as Virgin and Mother. This, too, bespeaks the "newness" of Jesus. Catholic doctrine teaches that Mary remained a virgin throughout her life. When we hear references in Scripture to Jesus' "brothers and sisters," we may think that Mary had other children after the birth of Jesus. However, these are rightly understood as close relatives of Christ, not his actual siblings (*Compendium*, 99). This is sometimes a point of discussion with some non-Catholic Christians who do not believe in Mary's perpetual virginity.

However, Mary's virginity and her motherhood are linked. In giving birth to her one son, the incarnate Son of God, Mary's pure love and spiritual motherhood extend to all whom Christ came to save. Far from being sterile, Mary's virginity is abundantly fruitful in bringing the Savior into the world and in helping us as members of the Church to live the new life that he has won for us. Indeed, Mary plays an essential role in God's plan of redemption. Not only did she bring the Savior into the world, but she is also the ultimate model of the Church, which is to be both virginal in the purity of her teaching and motherly in her love for all her sons and daughters.

The Mystery Hidden from Ages

And so the mysteries of Christ's infancy—such as the Epiphany, the presentation in the Temple, and the Holy Family's flight into and return from Egypt—bring us to the heart of the good news, "the mystery hidden from ages" but now newly and definitively revealed in Christ (Ephesians 3:9; *Compendium*, 103). In these events, the divinity of Jesus, born of Mary, shines through. In the household at Nazareth, something of Jesus' wondrous humanity can be glimpsed. We may learn much by mediating on the "hidden life" of Jesus and the simplicity, love, and obedience of the Holy Family (104).

To begin his public life and ministry, Jesus received John's baptism of repentance for the forgiveness of sins (Luke 3:3). Though he was sinless, Christ identified with all of humanity and, in so doing, was revealed as "the well-beloved Son" and "the Lamb of God, who takes away the sin of the world" (cf. Matthew 17:5; John 1:29). The liturgy tells us that Jesus, "the very author of Baptism," was baptized by John the Baptist to "make holy the flowing waters" (Preface, The Nativity of St. John the Baptist). In this way, Jesus' baptism prefigures our own baptism "by water and the Holy Spirit" (cf. John 3:5), through which we begin to participate in the new life that Jesus has won for us by his cross and resurrection.

Let us live joyfully the "newness" of life imparted to us. May the light of Christ shine ever more brightly in our hearts as we continue to meditate on the mystery of the Word made flesh.

For Personal Reflection and Group Discussion

1. How would you explain to non-Christians or atheists the scriptural statement that "there is no other name" than Jesus' by which we are to be saved (Acts 4:12, RSV)?

_____

_____

_____

_____

_____

2. In what ways is Christ utterly unique as Lord and Savior?

_____

_____

_____

_____

_____

3. Give several examples of why and how Mary's virginity is "fruitful" rather than sterile.

_____

_____

_____

_____

_____

4. Recall an occasion when you turned to Mary for her aid or experienced her spiritual motherhood. What impact did this have on you? What might you do to deepen your appreciation of Mary and your devotion to her?

_____

_____

_____

_____

_____

5. In what sense is Christ's life a mystery? Choose and discuss one of the events of Christ's infancy or public life, exploring its meaning and the truths that are revealed to us about him through it.

_____

_____

_____

_____

_____

12. Christ Gave Himself for Us

*THE SEASON OF LENT LEADS US TO REPENT AND
ENCOUNTER THE KINGDOM OF GOD*

Compendium: 106–111
Scripture Passage: Mark 1:12-15

There is no better time than Lent to meditate daily on the redemption that the Lord has won for us by his suffering, death, and resurrection. Lent is a time of renewal during which we ask for the grace to strengthen our prayer life, to practice fasting and mortification, and to give generously of ourselves to those in need. It is not a mere self-improvement program but a time-tested way of participating more deeply in Christ's sacrifice of love.

Throughout the season of Lent, the Church offers us encouragement to undergo a profound conversion from sin, which involves humbly and prayerfully coming to terms with our sinfulness and seeking forgiveness in sacramental Confession. In the joy of forgiveness, we are invited to share more deeply in the Father's merciful love.

On Ash Wednesday, we hear the invitation to repent, to believe in the gospel, and to become a part of the kingdom of God. Even the worst sinner is called to conversion (*Compendium*, 107). Christianity is replete with stories of hardened sinners who heard the Lord's call and reformed their lives. During Lent we should reflect on what areas of our lives are not under the merciful dominion of the Savior. In what specific ways do we need to repent?

For some, Lent is a time of intense final preparation for reception into the Church at the Easter Vigil. For most, however, it is about recovering one's baptismal innocence and hearing anew Christ's call to holiness. In either case, we must be attentive to the Scriptures proclaimed during the Sunday liturgy, for they echo Jesus' preaching of the kingdom of God.

Victory over Temptation

The Gospel reading for the First Sunday of Lent focuses on the temptations of Jesus in the desert (Matthew 4:1-11; Mark 1:12-13; Luke 4:1-13). Here we sense Christ's solidarity with us, since we face temptations every day. If we look deeper, we also sense Jesus' amazing holiness. The Letter to the Hebrews puts it this way: "For we do not have a high priest who is unable to sympathize with our weaknesses, but one who has similarly been tested in every way, yet without sin" (4:15). If we take yet a step further, we see the temptations of Jesus from the breathtaking panorama of salvation history. Christ's encounter with Satan in the desert sums up "the temptation of Adam in Paradise and the temptations of Israel in the desert" (*Compendium*, 106). Adam gave in to Satan's promptings, and the people of Israel succumbed to the lure of worshipping idols. In doing so, both disobeyed God.

In the Gospel accounts, we find Jesus in the desert, a place of desolation where the battle between God and Satan is set in sharp relief. Satan tries to deter Christ with lures that are familiar to us: self-indulgence, wealth, and power. Jesus resists Satan and thus foreshadows the victory he will win for us.

In Christ's victory over temptation, the light of hope is rekindled in our hearts. If we are one with him, can we not also live in such a way that the glory of God shines forth in our words and deeds and from the depths of our hearts? In this light, the Second Sunday of Lent is devoted each year to the Transfiguration. Jesus takes Peter, James, and John to the top of Mount Tabor, where he is transfigured as he speaks with Moses and Elijah (Matthew 17:1-8; Mark 9:2-8; Luke 9:28-36). Jesus fulfills in himself the law and the prophets—thus, the presence of Moses and Elijah—and reveals that his glory will be revealed definitively by his cross and resurrection.

How amazed Peter, James, and John must have been to see their Lord and Master transfigured before their eyes! And how encouraged we should be! The Church presents this mystery to open our eyes to the Lord's goodness and glory, which we are destined to share fully when Christ will "change our lowly body to be like his glorious body" (Philippians 3:21, RSV); *Compendium*, 110).

Signs and Wonders

During the remaining Sundays of Lent, the Church continues to present Jesus' preaching, together with his miracles. On the Third Sunday of Lent (Cycle A), we meet the Samaritan woman at the well (John 4:5-42), whose heart is opened as Jesus invites her to "worship in Spirit and truth" (4:24). The following Sunday we encounter the man born blind, a powerful symbol of our enlightenment in Christ. On the Fifth Sunday of Lent, we witness how Jesus raised Lazarus from the dead. During other years, the cycle of readings for the Lenten liturgies brings us Jesus' parable of the prodigal son (Luke 15:11-32), the story of the woman caught in adultery (John 8:1-11), and the story of the clandestine follower of Christ—Nicodemus—who discusses with Jesus the mysteries of the kingdom of God (John 3:1-21).

Jesus did not accompany his preaching with signs and wonders to amuse or amaze his audiences. Rather, his miracles were themselves announcements of the Good News (*Compendium*, 108). They did not portend an easy, pain-free life but served as indicators that Jesus had come to unleash into the world a love stronger than sin, a love that would ultimately conquer "Satan and all his works," as we say in our baptismal vows.

Throughout the liturgical year, we will meet the disciples of Jesus again and again and observe the ongoing formation of the apostles. Gradually, they will begin to share both in Christ's mission and in his authority to teach, forgive sins, and build up and guide the Church. In particular, Peter will confess Christ as "the Son of the living God" (Matthew 16:16). In spite of his weaknesses, Peter will come to embrace his mission, thus strengthening his brother apostles in their role of handing on the faith (*Compendium*, 109).

As Holy Week begins, we celebrate each year the triumphal entry of Jesus into Jerusalem (*Compendium,* 111). The liturgy presents for us the Messiah-King's arrival as he embraces his mission in loving obedience to the Father's saving will. Like the crowds in Jerusalem, we wave palm branches and proclaim him as our King: "Blessed is he who comes in the name of the Lord!" (Matthew 21:9). We sit at table with the Lord who gives himself as our food, we stand beneath the cross with Mary and John, and we stand watch at the tomb on the Easter Vigil as the light of Christ dawns upon us more brightly.

For Personal Reflection and Group Discussion

1. Examine your attitude toward Lent. Do you welcome the Lenten season as a time for deeper conversion and repentance, or do you approach it with dread or lethargy? What Lenten practices do you find most helpful?

   _____

   _____

   _____

   _____

   _____

2. How does the account of Jesus' victory over Satan tempting him in the wilderness give you hope for resisting temptations in your own life (Matthew 4:1-11; Mark 1:12-13; Luke 4:1-13)? How does the Sacrament of Reconciliation help you in resisting temptation?

   _____

   _____

   _____

   _____

3. In what ways do you think the Transfiguration was significant for Jesus himself? For Peter, James, and John? What does this scriptural event say to you personally?

_____

_____

_____

_____

_____

4. What is your favorite Lenten Gospel reading? Share about how that passage has impacted your life.

_____

_____

_____

_____

_____

5. Picture yourself among the crowds as Jesus entered Jerusalem on the first Palm Sunday (Matthew 21:1-11; Mark 11:1-11; Luke 19:29-44; John 12:12-19). How do you think you would have responded?

_____

_____

_____

_____

_____

13. The Paschal Mystery

In the Liturgy of Holy Week, We Commemorate Christ's
Passion, Death, and Resurrection

Compendium: 112–126
Scripture Passage: John 13:1

When I was in seminary, a professor exhorted me and my fellow classmates not to separate the "component parts" of the paschal mystery, which consists of Christ's suffering, death, resurrection, and exaltation. Rather, these events are united and stand at the center of our faith (*Compendium*, 112).

In order to understand what is meant by the term "paschal mystery," let us first look to the Old Testament. The word "paschal" comes from the Hebrew word meaning both "the passing over" and "passage." In the story of the exodus, the dramatic departure of the people of Israel from Egypt, the angel "passed over" the homes marked by the blood of the sacrificed paschal lamb, sparing the lives of the Israelites who then made the arduous passage from slavery to freedom (Exodus 12–14). The Israelites' celebration of this event would not only be the recollection of a historical event but a living memorial.

This first Pasch anticipated the definitive deliverance from sin that Christ, the Lamb of God, would win for us by shedding his blood (1 Corinthians 5:7). United to Christ in Baptism, we are to pass with Christ from the death of sin to new and eternal life.

Fulfillment of the Law

In embracing his mission to save us, Jesus entered the city of Jerusalem knowing that he would face accusations of disregarding the Law of Moses and of blaspheming by "making himself equal to God" (John

5:18; *Compendium*, 113–114). At a deeper level, he grasped that he was about to pour out his life in sacrificial love.

Paradoxically, Christ stood before his accusers as the fulfillment of the Law of Moses—indeed, as the new Moses who definitively interpreted the law and the prophets.

As the Son of God who assumed our humanity, Jesus was the fulfillment of all that God had promised his people. Yet God fulfilled his promises in such an unexpectedly marvelous way that Jesus was thought to be a blasphemer instead of the Savior (*Compendium*, 116).

It does not do, however, for us to impute the guilt for Jesus' death to those who historically brought about his death. On the contrary, we are all sinners, and Christ died because of our sins. As Christians who have experienced the love of Christ, we bear even greater responsibility when we fall into sin (*Compendium*, 117).

At the same time, we marvel at the loving initiative of the Father in sending us his Son (*Compendium*, 118). As St. John puts it, "In this is love: not that we have loved God, but that he loved us and sent his Son as expiation for our sins" (1 John 4:10). St. Paul writes, "But God proves his love for us in that while we were still sinners Christ died for us" (Romans 5:8). Was this not the goal of the Incarnation? Jesus assumed our humanity so that it might be the very means of our redemption.

If it is important for us not to separate the events of the paschal mystery, it is also important for us not to isolate the paschal mystery from the rest of Christ's life. "The entire life of Christ was a free offering to the Father to carry out his plan of salvation" (*Compendium*, 119). Jesus, God's incarnate Son, fulfilled his mission by announcing the kingdom, confirming his proclamation with miracles, and then taking upon himself our sins. In dying, he underwent the experience that most epitomizes our estrangement from God and from one another. By rising, he not only showed us the path to reconciliation, but he also enabled us to walk that path, thanks to "the love of God [that] has been poured out into our hearts through the holy Spirit" (Romans 5:5). This is how we must understand the great events of salvation that are re-presented and celebrated during Holy Week.

Love "to the End"

On Holy Thursday, we find ourselves, in a certain sense, at table with Christ and the apostles. On the eve of his suffering and death, Jesus signifies and makes truly present the total gift of self that he will make in his new definitive Pasch (*Compendium*, 120). Taking bread and wine, he says, "This is my body, which will be given for you" (Luke 22:19). "This is my blood . . . , which will be shed . . . for the forgiveness of sins" (Matthew 26:28). This is no mere sentimental gesture. When Jesus adds, "Do this in memory of me" (Luke 22:19), he commands the apostles not only to recall what he has done at the Last Supper, but also to reenact that same mystery of love (Acts 2:42). Thus, St. Paul teaches, "As often as you eat this bread and drink the cup, you proclaim the death of the Lord until he comes" (1 Corinthians 11:26). Here is the very origin of the Mass and the priesthood, given to us by Christ "on the night he was handed over" (11:23).

With majestic simplicity, the liturgy of Holy Week moves from the warmth of the upper room to the garden where "Jesus accepted the duty to carry our sins in his Body, 'becoming obedient unto death'" (*Compendium*, 121; cf. Philippians 2:8). Jesus' agony, like the entirety of his suffering and death, unmasked "the mystery of lawlessness" and the enormity of our sins (2 Thessalonians 2:7). As we behold the "author of life" (Acts 3:115) in agony, we should resolve not to trivialize our sins, a temptation that is all too common.

Having taken upon himself our sins, Jesus, the Lamb of God, offered his life to the Father. It was not that God the Father was angrily demanding the death of his own Son in reparation for our sins. Rather, Jesus' obedience is the key to our reconciliation with God and with those whom our sins harm. In looking upon the crucified, we consider the lengths to which God, in his love, went to save us. This is what St. John calls love "to the end" (John 13:1). In giving up his life in obedience to the Father's saving will, Jesus unleashed into the world a reconciling love that we are called to make our own. He asks us to take up our crosses and to associate ourselves with his sacrifice of love in the joys and sufferings of life (*Compendium*, 122–123).

As the passion account from John's Gospel is read on Good Friday, we should open our hearts in gratitude. We see in the blood and water from Christ's pierced side the fountain of the Church's sacramental life. We keep vigil with Mary at the foot of the cross and are heartened when Christ gives her as our mother through the apostle John. As Jesus truly dies and is buried, how we should be filled with wonder! Seamlessly, the sadness of Christ's death gives way to the joy of the resurrection as Easter dawns upon us (*Compendium*, 126).

For Personal Reflection and Group Discussion

1. Explain, in your own words, the meaning and importance of the paschal mystery of Jesus. What did Jesus accomplish for us through this mystery?

2. How is Jesus' sacrifice of his life for our sake expressed in the Last Supper? What fruits of his redemption have you experienced through receiving Jesus' Body and Blood in the Eucharist?

_____

_____

3. Which moment or event from Jesus' passion as recorded in the Gospels touches you most profoundly? Why?

_____

_____

_____

_____

_____

4. Jesus loved us "to the end" (John 13:1), giving his life and paying a tremendous price for our salvation. What response does this stir in you? What could you do to grow in loving Jesus more deeply?

_____

_____

_____

_____

5. How does your belief in Jesus' resurrection affect your outlook on your daily life? Do you fear your own death? Why or why not?

_____

_____

_____

_____

_____

14. "At the Right Hand of the Father"

THE RISEN LORD REMAINS PRESENT TO THE CHURCH TODAY AS WE WORK TO BUILD HIS KINGDOM ON EARTH

Compendium: 127–135
Scripture Passage: Ephesians 1:17-23

In one of his many homilies, St. Augustine warned his fifth-century congregation not to pine for the good old days: "You hear people complaining about this present day and age because things were so much better in former times!" (cited in the Office of Readings, Wednesday in Ordinary Time, Week IV).

He could easily be speaking to us. At one time or another, all of us have conjured up an imaginary time when life was better and discipleship was easier. Longing for the "good old days" indicates that we don't understand the hardships our forebears had to endure. Instead of waiting with "blessed hope," as we hear at Mass, we may find ourselves trying to turn back the clock—but time knows only one direction.

The First Disciples

If ever there was a group that needed faith and trust in God and his promises, it was the first followers of Christ. They truly lived in unprecedented times. They saw with their eyes and touched with their hands the Word made flesh. They witnessed Jesus' miracles, saw him die on the cross, and encountered him after he had risen.

We may wrongly imagine that faith came easily to these first Christians. Yet it is difficult to grasp how astonishing Christ's resurrection really was for his first disciples. "The apostles could not have invented the story of the resurrection since it seemed impossible to them" (*Compendium*, 127). They needed faith and trust in God no less than we do!

After all, the resurrection of Jesus was not merely a resuscitation; it was different from the miracles that Jesus had performed to bring the dead back to life. Like those miracles, Jesus' resurrection was an event in history, and the marks on his hands and side attest to the fact that "his risen body is that which was crucified" (*Compendium*, 129). Nonetheless, the resurrection was an event that goes beyond history. By rising from the dead, Jesus brought our humanity into the glory of God.

Scripture reveals that Jesus, risen from the dead, could "appear to his disciples how and where he wished and under various aspects" (*Compendium*, 129). Thus, Mary Magdalene thought Jesus was the gardener until he spoke her name (John 20:11-16). Similarly, the two disciples on the road to Emmaus did not recognize the risen Lord as they walked along; their eyes were opened when they recognized him in the breaking of bread (Luke 24:13-31). Finally, the apostles, locked in the upper room out of fear, were amazed when Jesus stood in their midst (24:36-43).

While these appearances and others after Christ's resurrection brought joy to the disciples, they also caused deep wonderment, fear, and confusion. After all, in the resurrection the disciples encountered the awesome work of the Holy Trinity. As the *Compendium* explains, "The three Persons act together according to what is proper to them: the Father manifests his power; the Son 'takes again' the life which he freely offered (John 10:17), reuniting his soul and his body which the Spirit brings to life and glorifies" (*Compendium*, 130).

In a very real sense, there was no road map for the life of faith that the first followers of Christ were called to embrace. The resurrection surpassed all that God had promised of old. To be one of these first disciples would certainly have been a challenge, the likes of which we can scarcely imagine. To be sure, the disciples fully came to grasp all of it only after they had received the Holy Spirit.

Looking into the Heavens

In some ways, of course, the resurrection confirmed that Jesus is truly the Son of God. It also confirmed all he had ever taught and done. As the victor over sin and death, Jesus makes it possible for us to stand holy and righteous before God as his beloved sons and daughters. We share his risen life now through the life of grace; we hope one day to share in the resurrection, when Christ "will raise up in the flesh those who have died, and transform our lowly body after the pattern of his own glorious body" (Eucharistic Prayer III; *Compendium*, 131).

On the Solemnity of the Ascension, we read how the disciples were "looking intently at the sky" after the Lord ascended (Acts 1:10). Naturally, they longed for the risen Lord to remain with them. Just as the Son of God descended into human history by becoming man, so now did he ascend, bearing on his shoulders a redeemed humanity.

Indeed, Jesus ascended beyond human sight to "the right hand of God" (Acts 2:33; cf. Ephesians 1:20-22). Echoing Psalm 16:11, St. Augustine teaches that God's right hand is a place of indescribable peace and joy. It is here that Jesus reigns, the supreme instrument of God's mighty hand (Psalm 80:16, 18). As we say at Mass, he is "seated at the right hand of the Father to intercede for us" (Penitential Rite, Form C).

Because he was God's Son who fulfilled the Father's plan of redemption, Jesus' saving deeds have universal value for every time, place, and culture. Even though he is exalted at the Father's right hand, Jesus also remains with us, just as he promised. By the power of the Holy Spirit, his kingdom of the Beatitudes takes root on earth through the ministry and sacramental life of the Church. It is this kingdom that we hope to experience fully in heaven.

Without presumption, we look ahead to the final judgment when "the secrets of hearts will be brought to light as well as the conduct of each one toward God and toward his neighbor" (*Compendium*, 135). We pray for Christ to come again, not only to reveal fully his glory, but, indeed, to be the judge of the living and dead. The fact of final judgment underscores the need for us not to dawdle in the past but, rather, to seek forgiveness, to live each day in love of God and neighbor, and to pray as men and women of hope, adopted sons and daughters of the heavenly Father. The prayer on our lips should be the same as the first Christians: "Come, Lord Jesus!" (Revelation 22:20).

For Personal Reflection and Group Discussion

1. In what way was Jesus' resurrection from the dead different from a resuscitation?

2. On what do you base your faith in Jesus' resurrection? Do you have difficulty believing in Jesus' resurrection? Why or why not?

3. How would you describe Jesus' glorified body after he rose from the dead? (Read Luke 24:36-40 and John 20:19-20 as you consider your answer.) How do you envision your own resurrected existence in heaven?

_____

_____

_____

_____

_____

4. At his ascension, Jesus promised his disciples, "I am with you always, until the end of the age" (Matthew 28:20). Speaking from your own experience, in what ways have you seen Jesus keeping this promise? Where do you recognize Jesus present in the world today?

_____

_____

_____

_____

_____

5. Describe and discuss Jesus' role as "seated at the right hand" of the Father. What significance does this have for your present life? For the final judgment?

_____

_____

_____

_____

_____

15. "I Believe in the Holy Spirit"

*THE THIRD PERSON OF THE HOLY TRINITY IS THE
"DRIVING FORCE" OF THE CHURCH'S LIFE*

Compendium: 136–146
Scripture Passage: John 14:16-17, 26

Every year on the Solemnity of Pentecost, we celebrate the coming of the Holy Spirit upon the apostles and the Blessed Virgin Mary, who were watching and waiting in prayer fifty days after Christ's resurrection. In this chapter, let's review the Church's teaching on the Holy Spirit.

We affirm that the Holy Spirit is the third Person of the Blessed Trinity. This does not mean that the Spirit is third in rank or importance, or that he came to exist at a later time. Rather, he is "third" because, as we say in the Nicene Creed, he eternally "proceeds from the Father and the Son." We profess that he is "worshipped and glorified with the Father and the Son," with whom he is coequal and coeternal (*Compendium*, 136).

Unfortunately, lifelong Catholics may think of the doctrine of the Trinity as needless mental gymnastics. Sometimes even theologians neglect it. Yet the fact is that the Holy Trinity and the work of the Holy Spirit are at the very heart of every aspect of our life of faith. While the Trinity remains a mystery of faith, it is a splendid, life-giving mystery—the secret of God's inward communion of life and love.

Blessed Paul VI memorably summarized this teaching in *Solemni Hac Liturgia* [Credo of the People of God]: "We believe then in the Father who eternally begets the Son; in the Son, the Word of God, who is eternally begotten; in the Holy Spirit, the uncreated Person who proceeds from the Father and the Son as their eternal Love" (10). We are destined to share fully in this communion, which we have already begun to possess through participation in the Church's life.

"The Giver of Life"

Unlike the eternal Word who became flesh, the Holy Spirit remains invisible. Yet we know the presence and power of the Spirit by his manifold works. It is the Spirit who allows us to be adopted sons and daughters of the heavenly Father, who opens our hearts in faith, and who sanctifies and guides us in the daily following of Christ. Likewise, it is the Holy Spirit who guides and acts in the Church's teaching office and sacramental life (*Compendium*, 137).

Before he ascended into heaven, Jesus promised the apostles "another Advocate" to guide them (John 14:16). While the third Person of the Trinity is most often referred to as the Holy Spirit in the teaching, worship, and devotional life of the Church, he has other titles as well. Other translations of John 14:16 use the word "Paraclete," "Counselor," or "Comforter." Throughout the New Testament, especially in the letters of Paul, we read about "the Spirit of Christ" (Romans 8:9). He is also referred to as "the Spirit of glory" and "the promise of the Spirit" (1 Peter 4:14; Galatians 3:14). In the Nicene Creed, we profess that he is "the Lord, the giver of life" (cf. Romans 8:11). These titles indicate the close interrelationship of the Holy Spirit with every aspect of Christ's Incarnation, life, teaching, miracles, and, most especially, his death and resurrection (*Compendium*, 138).

The Holy Spirit is also symbolized in many ways. For example, the Spirit is referred to as "*living water* which springs from the wounded Heart of Christ and which quenches the thirst of the baptized" (*Compendium*, 139; cf. John 19:34 and 1 John 5:8). In the Sacrament of Confirmation, the coming of the Spirit upon those to be confirmed is symbolized and accomplished by the laying on of hands and the anointing with holy oil or chrism (1 John 2:20; 2 Corinthians 1:21). St. Luke's account of Pentecost describes the Holy Spirit as "tongues as of fire" (Acts 2:3). And in the accounts of Christ's baptism, the Spirit descends as a dove (Matthew 3:13-17; Mark 1:9-11; *Compendium*, 139).

Although the truth of God's Triune life came to light only through Christ, the Old Testament prophets spoke under the Holy Spirit's influence (*Compendium*, 140). The last of the prophets, John the Baptist, stands at the frontier between the Old and New Testaments as the forerunner of Christ (Luke 1:17). He saw the Spirit descend upon Jesus in the waters of the Jordan and also prophesied that Jesus would baptize with the Holy Spirit (Matthew 3:16; John 1:33; *Compendium*, 141).

Just as marvelous was the work of the Holy Spirit in Mary. It was the Spirit of holiness who kept her free from sin in view of the saving work Jesus would accomplish. It was through the power of the Holy Spirit that she conceived and gave birth to the incarnate Son of God. And it was through the Spirit that she became the Mother of the whole Church.

The Outpouring of the Spirit

The Holy Spirit was poured out abundantly upon the apostles and the Virgin Mary as they prayed. The Church came to life as the living extension of the mission of Christ and the Spirit—namely, to lead all people to holiness and thus to communion with the Trinity. The Eastern liturgy summarizes this mystery admirably: "We have seen the true Light, we have received the heavenly Spirit, we have found the true faith: we adore the indivisible Trinity, who has saved us" (*Compendium*, 144).

The Church teaches that the Holy Spirit is the "soul" of the body of Christ, the Church. In that light we can understand what it means to say that the Spirit "animates and sanctifies the Church" (*Compendium*, 145; cf. CCC, 797). Indeed, as Pope Francis has said, the Holy Spirit is the "driving force" of the Church's life (General Audience, May 22, 2013). He enables us to pray and to proclaim the saving gospel of truth and love. The Spirit of love restores divine likeness in those who are baptized, confirms his gifts in those who become full members of the Church in Confirmation, empowers priests to bring forth the true and living presence of Christ in the Eucharist, imparts forgiveness in the Sacrament of Penance, and grants complementary vocations and gifts to the people of God. We bring forth a rich harvest of new life and love known as the "fruit" of the Holy Spirit when we open our hearts to his gifts (Galatians 5:22; *Compendium*, 145–146).

Let's ask for a fresh outpouring of the Holy Spirit upon the Church, upon our families, and upon our own life. United may we pray, "Come, Holy Spirit, and fill the hearts of your faithful!"

For Personal Reflection and Group Discussion

1. What do the titles "Paraclete," "Counselor," "Comforter," and "Advocate" for the Holy Spirit suggest to you about some aspects of the Spirit's role and function in the life of the Church? In your own life?

_____

_____

_____

_____

_____

2. How would you characterize your relationship with the Holy Spirit? Do you pray to the Spirit? What else might you do to deepen or enliven this relationship?

_____

_____

_____

_____

_____

3. What symbol for the Spirit is most meaningful to you personally? Why?

_____

_____

_____

_____

_____

4. Describe several ways in which the Spirit is the "driving force" of the Church.

_____

_____

_____

_____

_____

5. What impact has your reception of the Sacrament of Confirmation had on you? Which "fruit of the Spirit" is manifested in your daily life (Galatians 5:22)?

_____

_____

_____

_____

_____

16. "I Believe in the Holy Catholic Church"

THE CHURCH, THE BODY OF CHRIST, IS A SIGN OF THE KINGDOM OF GOD ON EARTH

Compendium: 147–160
Scripture Passage: 1 Corinthians 12:12-14, 26-27

At Pentecost, the Holy Spirit overshadowed the apostles and the Virgin Mary, and the Church's mission began in earnest. Henceforth, Christ lives and acts in and with his Church, especially through the preaching of the word of God and the celebration of the sacraments. The Church will come to fulfillment when, at the end of time, she is gathered in exultant glory around the throne of the Triune God.

In the New Testament, the Greek word for church, *ekklesia*, is used 114 times—65 times by St. Paul alone. The *Compendium* tells us that this word "refers to the people whom God calls and gathers together from every part of the earth." To be sure, it is more than a group of like-minded people gathered together to support a cause. Rather, it is an assembly of faith and worship made up of those "who through faith and Baptism have become children of God, members of Christ, and temples of the Holy Spirit" (*Compendium*, 147). As "members of Christ," we are to glorify God by living our vocation, faithfully and robustly, for the common good.

There are many beautiful images of the Church found in the New Testament that have their roots in the Old Testament and that have attained fulfillment in Christ. As we will see, these images fit together and highlight a particular facet of the mystery of the Church (*Compendium*, 148).

Human and Divine

Jesus summarizes the mission of the Church entrusted to the apostles in these words: "Go, therefore, and make disciples of all nations, baptizing them in the name of the Father, and of the Son, and of the holy Spirit, teaching them to observe all that I have commanded you" (Matthew 28:19-20). In preaching the word and baptizing, the Church seeks to spread the kingdom of God among all the nations of the earth. The preface for the Solemnity of Our Lord Jesus Christ, King of the Universe, describes this kingdom (for which we pray daily when we recite the Our Father) as "a kingdom of truth and life, a kingdom of holiness and grace, a kingdom of justice, love and peace."

The Church, however, does not only *point* to the kingdom of God. Rather, the Church *is* the kingdom of God in seed form. Her mission is to engender the kingdom of God within each of us so that we may live in "righteousness, peace, and joy in the holy Spirit" (Romans 14:17). At the same time, the Church is an effective sign and instrument in accomplishing God's work of delivering the human family "from the power of darkness" and transferring us "to the kingdom of his beloved Son" (Colossians 1:13). Thus, we speak of the Church as "the universal sacrament of salvation" and as a "mystery" in the sense that her spiritual dimension can only be understood by faith (*Compendium*, 151–152).

Today it is common to separate the so-called institutional Church from the so-called spiritual Church. To be sure, aspects of the Church's visible institutional life are continually in need of reform. Yet it is also true that the visible day-to-day life of the Church is deeply connected to the Church's mission to transmit divine truth and life. Indeed, the Second Vatican Council and the *Catechism* explicitly warn against the error of separating the visible and invisible elements of the Church's mission (*Lumen Gentium* 8; CCC, 771). There is only one Church, comprised of human and divine elements. The visible is the sign of the invisible; the human is the sign of the divine.

We can see the significance of the Church as the living sign and instrument of God's kingdom when we reflect on the Church as the people of God. While we are each rightly concerned for our individual salvation, we are not saved "in isolation"(*Compendium*, 153), but rather as part of God's people. The Church as the people of God "has for its *origin* God the Father; for its *head* Jesus Christ; for its *hallmark* the dignity and freedom of the sons of God; for its *law* the new commandment of love; for its *mission* to be the salt of the earth and the light of the world; and for its *destiny* the Kingdom of God already begun on earth" (154). As members of this people, we come to share in Christ's role as priest, prophet, and king. We participate in Jesus' priestly, prophetic, and kingly office by offering ourselves, body and soul, as a spiritual sacrifice to God, by bearing witness to our faith before the world, and by serving the needs of others (155).

Body, Bride, and Temple

The principal image of the Church in the writings of St. Paul is the "body of Christ," which describes the solidarity of the members of the Church, through whom Christ acts. Just as the human body has many members with different functions, so it is with Christ and his body, the Church. Each member is to contribute to the life of the Church according to his or her vocation and out of concern for the common good. Just as the fullness of divinity is found in Christ, the head of this body, so too are its members filled with divine life. Christ's spirit is the animating principle. Indeed, so close is the union of head and members that St. Augustine spoke of the "whole Christ," and St. Thomas Aquinas wrote, "Head and members form, as it were, one and the same mystical person" (*Compendium*, 156–157).

Another beautiful image of the Church is the "bride of Christ," found principally in the writings of St. Paul but also in the Gospel of Mark (2:19). This image draws on Old Testament passages that speak of the Lord's spousal love for his people, Israel. In Ephesians

5:22 and following, St. Paul uses the relationship of husband and wife to show how deeply Christ loves the Church to whom he has joined himself in an everlasting covenant. His purifying and life-giving love has made the Church the mother of God's children (*Compendium*, 158).

A final image to be considered here is the Church as temple of the Holy Spirit. As noted earlier, the Holy Spirit dwells within the Church as her animating principle, or "soul." Thanks to the presence of the Spirit who raised Jesus from the dead, the Church grows as a place of faith, worship, and service constructed of living stones. It is built up by preaching the word of God, by the sacraments, by virtue, and by charisms, those "special gifts of the Holy Spirit which are bestowed on individuals for the good of others" (*Compendium*, 160).

We give thanks for the Church as "a people made one with the unity of the Father, the Son, and the Holy Spirit" (*Lumen Gentium*, 4, quoting St. Cyprian). May the Lord bless the Church and her members!

For Personal Reflection and Group Discussion

1. In what concrete ways do you experience being a member of the Church, the body of Christ? In what way do you contribute to the life of the Church?

_____

_____

_____

_____

_____

2. What does it mean that the Church is the kingdom of God "in seed form"?

_____

_____

_____

_____

_____

3. How do you participate in the mission of the Church to proclaim the kingdom of God? To be "salt" and "light" to the world?

_____

_____

_____

_____

_____

4. How do you share personally in the priestly, prophetic, and kingly functions of Christ?

_____

_____

_____

_____

_____

5. Which image of the Church—body of Christ, bride of Christ, temple of the Holy Spirit—speaks to you the most? Why?

_____

_____

_____

_____

17. "One, Holy, Catholic and Apostolic"

THE FOUR MARKS OF THE CATHOLIC CHURCH ARE ESSENTIAL TO UNDERSTANDING THE BODY OF CHRIST

Compendium: 161–176
Scripture Passage: Matthew 28:19-20

In the Nicene Creed, we profess our belief in the Church as "one, holy, catholic and apostolic." In order to understand the Church, we need to recognize these four essential attributes, or "marks."

Let us begin with the unity or oneness of the Church. Regrettably, we often hear about the Church's *disunity*. Of course, we are aware of divisions within the Catholic Church: some are stylistic, others substantive, and still others are the result of human discord. In addition, we are aware that we are separated from other Christians. So how can we speak of the Church as "one"?

As noted previously, we need to begin with the source of our unity, namely, the one God in three divine Persons. St. Cyprian of Carthage described the Church as "a people made one with the unity of the Father, the Son, and the Holy Spirit" (cited in *Lumen Gentium*, 4). The Church is made up of many members, but she is united by the Holy Spirit, who brings God's people together in communion. As the *Compendium* puts it, "The Church has but one faith, one sacramental life, one apostolic succession, one common hope, and one and the same charity" (161).

Unified and Holy

It is sometimes said that God's gift of unity can be found in the spiritual core of the Church but not in her visible existence. The Church herself steers us away from this false idea. The Second Vatican Council restated that "the one Church of Christ, as a society constituted and organized in the world, subsists in (*subsistit in*) the Catholic Church, governed by the Successor of Peter and the bishops in communion with him" (*Compendium*, 162). The phrase "subsists in" may sound unusual but was chosen carefully. It means that in spite of the problems and divisions caused by human frailty and sinfulness, there is to be found in the Church the fullness of truth, sacramental life, and communion.

In addition, the phrase "subsists in" helps us see how we can recognize the "many elements of sanctification and truth" found in church communities not in full communion with the Catholic Church (*Compendium*, 163). This recognition is not meant to downplay serious differences among Christian communities but rather to underline the inner requirement of the Church to seek the unity that Christ willed for his followers. We must all pray and work for this unity by deepening our communion with Christ and his Church, as well as by respectful theological dialogue (164). Taken together, this graced effort to seek Christian unity is called "ecumenism."

We also profess our faith in the Church as "holy." Once again, we recognize that not all members of the Church, including ourselves, are holy; we all stand in need of forgiveness. Happily, in God's eyes we are more than the sum of our sins and failures, and the Church, more than the sum of her members, shares in the holiness of God. As St. Paul teaches, Christ gave himself up for the Church and her sanctification (Ephesians 5:22-27; *Compendium*, 165). The Church, therefore, provides all that we need to respond to the call to holiness.

In a particular way, the Church's holiness is found in the saints. With Mary leading the way, the saints not only show us how to participate in God's truth, goodness, and love, but they also support us by their prayers.

Universal and Apostolic

Next, we proclaim that the Church is "catholic," or universal. In the Gospel of Matthew, we read that following the resurrection, Jesus sent the apostles to preach the gospel in every corner of the world and to baptize all peoples in the name of the Trinity (28:19). At the same time, Jesus commissioned the apostles to teach all nations "all that I have commanded you" (Matthew 28:20; *Compendium*, 172). From the very beginning, the Church was catholic because her mission was to all nations and was entrusted with the totality of the Christian faith (166). As the faith spread, the Church was organized into dioceses or eparchies, which are presided over by bishops in union with the bishop of Rome (the pope). We sense the universality of each particular church during the Eucharistic Prayer at Mass when we pray in union with the Church "throughout the world."

Obviously, not everyone considers himself to be a member of the Church. Nonetheless, every person is called to share in "the Catholic unity of the people of God" (*Compendium*, 168). Some Catholics, of course, are initiated into the Church but do not practice their faith. Practicing Catholics must seek to spread the gospel by word and example, working with pastors to encourage non-practicing Catholics to return to their faith (173). Meanwhile, the baptized who belong to other Christian churches "do not enjoy full Catholic unity" but "are in a certain, although imperfect, communion with the Catholic Church" (168). We are called to foster unity with these Christians and to bear witness to the fullness of our Catholic faith.

In addition, the Church recognizes in a special way that God revealed himself to the Jewish people and made them his own; they were the first to receive his word, setting them apart from all other non-Christian religions (*Compendium*, 169). Still, the Church recognizes in other non-Christian religions elements that reflect God's truth and goodness. We must seek to foster understanding with followers of those religions for the common good and as a way of bringing about "the unity of humanity in the Church of

Christ" (170). Through no fault of their own, many people have not received the gospel of Christ and his Church. While Christ is the source of all salvation, non-Christians can cooperate with grace and be saved if they sincerely seek God and strive to follow their consciences. On the other hand, those who know that the Church founded by Christ is necessary for salvation but choose to remain outside or apart from her imperil their salvation (171).

Finally, we profess our faith in the Church as "apostolic." This means several things: Christ founded the Church upon the apostles (Ephesians 2:20), the Church adheres to and hands on the teaching of the apostles, and the Church is apostolic in her structure—since the bishops are the successors to the apostles in communion with the successor of St. Peter (*Compendium*, 174). In the New Testament, we read how Jesus chose the apostles and formed them. They were witnesses to the resurrection. As the word "apostle" itself indicates, they were "sent" by Christ into the world to proclaim the gospel (175). By means of the Sacrament of Holy Orders, "the mission and power of the Apostles" is transmitted to their successors, the bishops. In this way, through the centuries, the Church remains linked to her apostolic faith, mission, and origins (176).

For Personal Reflection and Group Discussion

1. In spite of various sorts of division within the Church, how can we speak of it as "one"? What is the source of the unity of the Church?

_____

_____

_____

_____

_____

2. In what ways do you work to foster ecumenism and restore unity among Christians? How might you bear witness to the fullness of the Catholic faith?

_____

_____

_____

_____

_____

3. Why is it true and thus possible to say that the Church is "holy"? What marks of holiness do you recognize in the Church? In your own life?

_____

_____

_____

_____

_____

4. What is the relationship and connection of the Jewish faith with the faith of the Church?

_____

_____

_____

_____

_____

5. Why do we profess our faith in the Church as "apostolic"? How is the Church today still fulfilling the calling and mission of the apostles?

_____

_____

_____

_____

_____

18. The Christian Faithful

INSTITUTED BY CHRIST, THE HIERARCHY AND VISIBLE STRUCTURE OF THE CHURCH ARE PART OF GOD'S PLAN

Compendium: 177–193
Scripture Passage: Matthew 16:18-19

In companies an organized structure is intended to foster unity and encourage teamwork. Likewise, members of a loving family have varying roles and responsibilities that are complementary and contribute to the unity of the family and to the common good.

Something similar can be said of the visible structure of the Church, which has its origin in Christ. St. Paul taught us to see how varying vocations, ministries, and gifts of the Holy Spirit work together in love to build up the body of Christ. These vocations exist for the unity and common good of God's family.

The members of the Church, called "the Christian faithful," are those incorporated into Christ by Baptism and who thus become a part of the "people of God"—a phrase that has its roots in the Old Testament notion of the chosen people. In fulfillment of God's promises, Christ established the new and definitive covenant in his blood. The baptized partake in Christ's sacrifice of love and are called to proclaim and live the truth of the gospel. This call to holiness is universal. We speak, therefore, of "a true equality" among all members of the Church "in their dignity as children of God" (*Compendium*, 177).

Holy Orders

Among the different vocations, "by divine institution there exist *sacred ministers* who have received the Sacrament of Holy Orders and who form the hierarchy of the Church" (*Compendium*, 178). These ordained ministers include bishops, priests, and deacons. Christ instituted the Church hierarchy to nurture his people in truth and love. He chose, called, and formed the apostles. Above all, Jesus sent the Holy Spirit upon them and commanded them to feed his flock. In exercising their ministry, bishops and priests speak and act in the very Person of Christ so as to nourish Christ's people with his own divine life. Deacons serve God's people by preaching and teaching the word, by assisting in the liturgy, and by charity, especially in serving the poor and needy (179).

As successors to the apostles, bishops are called to serve in a unity of faith and love as part of the worldwide college of bishops in communion with the Holy Father. Priests are the closest co-workers of bishops. They exercise their priesthood as part of the "presbyterate" of a diocese, united with their fellow priests "in communion with their own bishop and under his direction" (*Compendium*, 180).

We recall that Jesus appointed St. Peter as head of the apostles. His successors—the popes down through the ages—are "the visible source and foundation of the unity of the Church" (*Compendium*, 182). As Vicar of Christ and head of the college of bishops, the pope manifests, embodies, and fosters the unity that the Lord willed for his followers. The pope is the supreme pastor of God's people and by God's will exercises "supreme, immediate, and universal power" over the whole Church (182). The college of bishops, always in union with the pope, "also exercises supreme and full authority over the Church" (183). Every diocese is a local manifestation of the universal Church, and the diocesan bishop governs with a view toward the good of the Church as a whole. Thus, the Church is like the interconnected parts of a single living organism.

The Magisterium

In union with the Holy Father, bishops exercise a threefold office of teaching, sanctifying, and governing. By teaching, together with priests, bishops lead people to explicit faith, to the sacraments, and to obedience to Christ's commandment of love.

The baptized, for their part, have received from the Holy Spirit a supernatural sense of the faith, which helps them accept and live the faith in accordance with the Magisterium, the living teaching office of the Church (*Compendium*, 184). The Magisterium is charged with authentically interpreting God's word in Scripture and Tradition, and serves to ensure that the faith of the apostles is handed on. The Church's Magisterium is at the service of the word of God.

Sometimes this teaching office is exercised infallibly, such as when the pope and the college of bishops definitively proclaim a doctrine regarding faith or morals. The faithful are to accept such teaching with the obedience of faith (*Compendium*, 185). Even when doctrines are not infallibly proclaimed, they are to be accepted with "religious submission of intellect and will" by all members of the Church (*Lumen Gentium*, 25). We may find the words "religious submission of mind and will" unattractive and authoritarian. Yet they must be understood in the context of love. Once we have fallen in love with God and have become disciples of the Lord Jesus, then we "hand over" our lives to him, only to have them filled with his truth and love, with spirit and life. Dissent from the Church's teaching often short-circuits the process of growing in missionary discipleship.

Laity and Consecration

Most members of the Church belong to the laity, a term that comes from the Greek word for "people." While members of the laity participate in the pastoral life of the Church, their principal vocation is to foster the growth of the kingdom of God in this world even while looking forward in hope to eternal life. With reason illuminated by faith, they seek to build a civilization of love in accordance with God's plan (*Compendium*, 188). The laity also shares in the priestly, prophetic, and kingly office of Christ. Often, this is done by parents who teach their children the faith or by the quiet but effective witness of a holy life at home and in the workplace.

Last, but surely not least, are those members of the faithful, both ordained and lay, called to consecrated ("religious") life. These men and women take vows and dedicate their lives to God by the evangelical counsels of chastity, poverty, and obedience. They often live in common, wear some form of distinctive dress (habit), and pursue a common apostolate, such as teaching, health care, service to the poor, or a life of contemplative prayer. By their way of life, the consecrated faithful foretell the perfection of love that awaits us in heaven. They lead all members of the Church to greater holiness and dedication to Christ and to his mission (*Compendium*, 192–193).

For Personal Reflection and Group Discussion

1. Why is there equality among all members of the Church, laity and hierarchy?

_____

_____

_____

_____

_____

2. How does the Church benefit from the office and ministry of its "sacred ministers," the ecclesiastical hierarchy (bishops, priests, deacons)?

_____

_____

_____

_____

_____

3. Discuss the significance of the pope being the "successor of Peter." What unique position and responsibilities does the pope hold within the Church?

_____

_____

_____

_____

_____

4. What is your attitude toward the Magisterium of the Church? Do you find it difficult to believe and submit to the teachings of the Church? Why or why not?

_____

_____

_____

_____

_____

5. What is the principal vocation of the laity? How do you see yourself fulfilling this role in your everyday life?

_____

_____

_____

_____

_____

19. Communion, Forgiveness, and Life Everlasting

Concluding the Creed, We Profess Our Belief in the Communion of Saints, Baptism, and the Final Resurrection

Compendium: 194–217

Scripture Passage: 1 Corinthians 15:51-57

It is often said that "the people" should have a greater say in how the Church is run. Of course, pastors, including bishops and parish priests, should listen to their people, tap into their expertise, and involve them deeply in the Church's life. But who are "the people"? We need to include all who belong to the Church's communion.

We acknowledge this in the Apostles' Creed when we say, "I believe in . . . the communion of saints." The *Compendium* explains the meaning of this phrase. First, the word "communion" implies that "all the members of the Church [share] in holy things: the faith, the sacraments, especially the Eucharist, the charisms, and the other spiritual gifts" (194). God's generous love, communicated by the Holy Spirit, brings us together. In this love, God invites us to share in his inner life. Rooted in Trinitarian love, we, the members of the Church, are called not to seek our own interests, but to place ourselves at the service of one another, especially the poor and needy (1 Corinthians 13:5).

The word "saints" in this context refers not only to those who have been canonized, but also to all the members of the Church—living and deceased—who are on their way to holiness, including those undergoing the final purification of purgatory. We should pay close attention to the example of the saints in heaven and seek their prayers, and we should also pray for those in purgatory. Both the living and the dead "form in Christ one family, the Church, to the praise and glory of the Trinity" (*Compendium*, 195).

Mary, Mother of the Church

The most important member of the communion of saints is Mary, the mother of Christ and Mother of the Church. Mary gave birth to Jesus and shared in his sacrifice. While dying on the cross, Jesus entrusted his mother to his disciples with the words "Behold, your mother" (John 19:27). Mary is thus "recognized as mother of salvation, life and grace"—indeed, the "Mother of the Church" (St. John Paul II, General Audience, September 17, 1997; *Compendium*, 196).

Mary's maternal care for the Church was evident from the beginning. After the ascension of Christ, she prayed with the apostles as they awaited the coming of the Holy Spirit (Acts 2:42). She also must have been present with the early Christians during their celebrations of the Eucharist (St. John Paul II, *Ecclesia de Eucharistia* [On the Eucharist in Its Relationship to the Church], 53).

Mary's example of faith and charity continues to shine upon the Church today. The Virgin Mary prays with and for the Church, and she is always mentioned in the Eucharistic Prayer at Mass. Filled with the saving power of Christ's love, she encourages us to grow in holiness. This is why we often turn to Mary as our advocate and helper, and why the Church encourages warm devotion to her (*Compendium*, 197).

Sometimes people incorrectly claim that Catholics "worship" Mary. We worship only the Trinity. However, we do have a special veneration for Mary because of her unique role in our salvation. We express this veneration by celebrating beautiful Marian liturgical feasts and by praying the Rosary, which has been described as "a compendium of the whole Gospel" (*Compendium*, 198). As we pray to Mary for her intercession, we see in her the perfection to which we should aspire as we journey toward heaven (199).

Our Catholic faith teaches us that Mary, in view of the merits of her son, was uniquely preserved from all sin from the moment of her conception. Yet we also profess in the Nicene Creed our belief in "one Baptism for the forgiveness of sins." Indeed, "The first and chief sacrament for the forgiveness of sins is Baptism" (*Compendium*, 200). Christ instituted the Sacrament of Reconciliation, or Penance, for sins committed after Baptism. The Church has the authority to forgive because Christ imparted the Holy Spirit upon the apostles and said, "Whose sins you forgive are forgiven them, and whose sins you retain are retained" (John 20:23).

The Last Things

The closing sentences of the Nicene Creed look at the "last things"—death, resurrection, judgment, and eternal destiny. Even though we sometimes try to forget, we need to reflect on what awaits us at the end of life. Death is not the last word; we are created to share in the resurrection of Christ. The separation of our bodies from our souls at death will not last for all eternity. In a manner we cannot now imagine, even our mortal bodies will be raised and reunited to our souls. The good will share in the resurrection of life; the wicked will share in the resurrection of condemnation (John 5:29; *Compendium*, 202–205). Each day we seek to live in Christ so that when we die, we will die in the Lord unto life everlasting (206).

At death we will each enter into eternity and undergo the "particular judgment" (*Compendium*, 208). We have our "definitive meeting with Christ" concerning our eternal destiny. Those who die in the grace of Christ and have no further need of purification share the happiness of heaven. Others die in God's friendship but need further purification, a state that is called "purgatory." We can help our sisters and brothers in purgatory by having Masses offered for them and by our prayers, good works, and personal sacrifices offered in Christ (*Compendium*, 209–211).

For those who die in mortal sin of their own free choice, hell consists in separation from God for whose love we were made. God takes no pleasure in the condemnation of sinners, yet he respects our freedom. If we choose to be separated from God in this life, we run the risk of being separated from God for all eternity (*Compendium*, 212–214).

The final and general judgment will occur, as we say in the Nicene Creed, when Christ "will come again in glory to judge the living and the dead." If we are truly living in Christ, we look forward to Christ's coming in joyful hope. We do not know when Christ's Second Coming will occur, so we live in both vigilance and hope. We should ask to share his life so completely that we contribute to that moment when God's plan of salvation will come to completion, and then, in eternity, God will be "all in all" (1 Corinthians 15:28; *Compendium*, 215–216).

To the profession of faith that we have now studied throughout the previous chapters, we add our "amen"—a Hebrew word that indicates our total assent to what the Church believes and teaches.

For Personal Reflection and Group Discussion

1. What is the meaning of the "communion of saints"? Explain what the word "communion" implies in this context.

_____

_____

_____

_____

_____

2. How does the communion of saints extend beyond the living? How do the saints help you in your life in Christ?

_____

_____

_____

_____

_____

3. Why is Mary recognized as the most important member of the communion of saints? How does she fulfill her maternal role toward the Church?

_____

_____

_____

_____

_____

4. Are you fearful of dying and so avoid thinking about your own death and Christ's judgment? As believers, how can we live in vigilance and hope rather than in fear of Christ's final coming?

_____

_____

_____

_____

_____

5. This week help your sisters and brothers in purgatory by offering Mass, prayers, good works, and personal sacrifices in Christ for them. Make it a more frequent practice to intercede for those in purgatory.

_____

_____

_____

_____

_____

20. Worshipping in Spirit and in Truth

*GOING TO MASS IS MUCH MORE THAN JUST
AN OBLIGATION FOR FAITHFUL CATHOLICS*

Compendium: 218–223
Scripture Passage: Matthew 26:26-28

Sometimes the liturgy is thought of only as outward ceremony. A friend of mine who does not practice the faith once said, "I get along fine without all the falderal!"—meaning the way in which the Mass and the sacraments are celebrated. "Real Christianity," he went on to say, "has to do with helping others." He speaks for many others. With that in mind, let us now turn our attention to reflecting on the Church's liturgy in order to deepen our understanding of it. The word "liturgy" comes from an ancient Greek word meaning "public service." In general, it refers to the public prayer of the Church, such as the Mass and the sacraments. Delving into the Church's Sacred Tradition, however, Pope Pius XII and the Second Vatican Council gave us a deeper understanding of the word "liturgy," which is reflected in the *Compendium*.

"Source and Summit"

The liturgy is, above all, the celebration of the paschal mystery—Christ's death and resurrection. It is the highest and best means by which Christ, our high priest, continues to act on our behalf to sanctify us, redeem us from our sins, and enable us to share in the life of God, both as individuals and as members joined together in the Church, the body of Christ. These outward signs, which are an essential part of the Church's ceremonies, show us how Christ sanctifies us and are also the effective means by which he does so. Sharing in the holiness of Christ, the head of the Church, we are united as members of his body in offering God fitting and acceptable worship (*Compendium*, 218).

Thus, we can readily understand why the liturgy is so important to the Church's life and mission. It is the font from which the Church continually receives Christ's saving power, which is utterly necessary for her mission to proclaim the gospel and to lead all people to salvation. The Church gives honor and glory to God by gathering people everywhere to share in what Christ has done to save us through the liturgy, "the summit toward which the activity of the Church is directed" (*Compendium*, 219).

Hand in hand with the liturgy is the phrase "sacramental economy." We are familiar with the word "sacrament" and the word "economy," but many are not familiar with the combination of the two. First, recall that a sacrament is an effective sign of God's grace entrusted to the Church by Christ. Among other things, economy refers to how wealth, the fruit of human labor, is distributed nationally and globally. In the economy of God's saving plan, the sacraments, and especially the Eucharist, are the means by which the fruits of Christ's saving work are extended and distributed among God's people "until he comes" (*Compendium*, 220). Of course, the liturgy and sacramental economy are interrelated: sacramental economy dispenses among the faithful the fruit of the saving events that the liturgy celebrates and makes present.

God's Work

All too often we think of the liturgy as something we do for God. But in fact the liturgy is first and foremost the work of the Trinity—Father, Son, and Holy Spirit. We see the role of each Person of the Trinity by considering the prayers of the liturgy itself.

Most liturgical prayers are addressed to God the Father. The Church begs the Father that we might share, through the power of the Holy Spirit, in what Christ has done to save us. Through the liturgy, the Father "fills us with his blessings in the Word made flesh who died and rose for us and pours into our hearts the Holy Spirit" (*Compendium*, 221). Filled with these blessings from above, we ascend in worship, praise, and thanksgiving to God, the Father of life and love.

The second Person of the Trinity, Christ, the Son of God made man, is our great high priest who acts on our behalf in and through the liturgy. The "work" that Christ accomplishes in the Mass and sacraments is the re-presentation of the paschal mystery. In other words, the mystery of love at the heart of God's plan for the world's salvation—the suffering, death, and resurrection of Christ—is "signified and made present" in and through the liturgy (cf. *Compendium*, 222). This means that the words and gestures of the liturgy not only remind us of Christ's saving words and deeds, but also make them present and active in our midst. How does this happen? "By giving the Holy Spirit to his apostles [Christ] entrusted to them and their successors the power to make present the work of salvation through the Eucharistic sacrifice and the sacraments" (222). In the power of the Holy Spirit, Christ acts through sacramental signs to give grace—a sharing in divine life—to his people of every time and place.

Finally, we should have the highest appreciation for the work of the Holy Spirit in the liturgy and the Church's sacramental life. As we have seen, the Holy Spirit is the soul of the Church and thus her living memory. The Spirit prompts the Church to ponder, like Mary, the events or mysteries of Christ's life in her heart; recalls and re-presents Christ to the members of the Church already enlightened by faith; makes Christ truly present; unites the Church to Christ and his mission; and makes the gift of her union with Christ bear abundant fruit in the Church and in the world (*Compendium*, 223).

May we allow the Holy Spirit to deepen in us the new life Christ has won for us by his death and resurrection so that we may truly worship the Father "in Spirit and truth" (John 4:24).

For Personal Reflection and Group Discussion

1. Why is the liturgy called "the source and summit" of the Church's life and mission? Share a personal experience that has underscored how meaningful the liturgy is to you.

   _____

   _____

   _____

   _____

   _____

2. Summarize briefly and discuss the meaning of "sacramental economy."

   _____

   _____

   _____

   _____

   _____

3. How are the fruits of Christ's redemption communicated to us? In what way is Christ at work in the liturgy?

   _____

   _____

   _____

   _____

   _____

4. Reflect on the various sacraments that you have received. Choose one, and share about its impact on your life.

_____

_____

_____

_____

_____

5. How aware of and attentive are you to the Holy Spirit's role in the liturgy and sacramental life of the Church? What could you do to increase your appreciation for the work of the Spirit?

_____

_____

_____

_____

_____

21. Celebrating the Church's Liturgy

*THE SACRAMENTS OF THE CHURCH BOTH SIGNIFY AND
MAKE PRESENT GOD'S TRANSFORMING GRACE*

Compendium: 224–249
Scripture Passage: Revelation 7:9-11

The first Christmas night was a scene of worship: Mary and Joseph worshipped the child given to them by God the Father through the Holy Spirit. The angels sang, "Glory to God!" and the shepherds gazed upon the newborn in wonder and awe.

Thanks to the sacramental and liturgical life of the Church, the truth and beauty of that first Christmas night, and indeed all the events of Christ's life, are not a dim memory but a present reality. As St. Leo the Great taught in the fifth century, "What was visible in our Savior has passed over into his mysteries" (*Compendium*, 225). We have a living contact with Christ through the seven sacraments, which Christ instituted and entrusted to the Church. The Church celebrates these sacraments and is built up by them (226).

The sacraments are efficacious signs through which God wishes to touch and transform our lives. For now, let us remember that three sacraments—Baptism, Confirmation, and Holy Orders—impart a sacramental character or spiritual "seal." Each of these three sacraments can be received only once because they permanently transform the recipient and "configure" him or her to Christ. This means that the Holy Spirit brings about in the depth of one's soul a spiritual image of Christ coupled with a participation in his life. In Baptism and Confirmation, this indelible seal marks out the recipient as an adopted son or daughter in Christ, a person both prepared and obligated to take part in the Church's worship. Holy Orders imparts a further sacramental character, enabling the ordained to act in the Person of Christ in the celebration of the liturgy (*Compendium*, 227; 235).

Signs of Grace

The sacraments express and fulfill Christ's promise to remain with his Church. This is the context in which we can most readily understand the Church's teaching. The sacraments do not simply illustrate God's grace; they are also the means through which the transforming power of grace is made available and active in our lives. Christ was so determined to remain with us in this way that the effectiveness of the sacraments does not depend on the personal worthiness of the minister performing them. Rather, "the sacraments are efficacious *ex opere operato* ('by the very fact that the sacramental action is performed')" (*Compendium*, 229).

This, however, leads to two other important considerations. First, anyone who performs a sacramental action, such as baptizing or celebrating Mass, has a most serious obligation to be in a state of grace and to pursue personal holiness rooted in the fullness of the Church's faith and moral teaching. Second, the sacraments need to be received with a living and active faith. When we approach the sacraments with faith, we find that they express, nourish, and strengthen our adherence to the faith of the Church. In fact, there is a deep and mutual correspondence between what we believe and how we worship (*Compendium*, 228).

At this point, we can begin to see that "for believers the sacraments . . . are necessary for salvation" (CCC, 1129). Through the sacraments we receive sacramental grace and forgiveness of our sins; we become the adopted children of God; we grow in likeness to Christ; and we become living members of his body, the Church (*Compendium*, 230). By sharing in the sacramental signs, we long to see God in heaven with all the redeemed and to rejoice in his presence forever (232).

The sacraments should not be understood to operate mechanistically. To the contrary, they are celebrated in the sacred rites or ceremonies known as the liturgy, the public prayer of the Church (see chapter 20). This prayer spans heaven and earth and is shared with Mary, the saints, and the angels (*Compendium*, 234). The Church's sacramental life has an inner beauty and logic all its own that emerges when it is celebrated faithfully, prayerfully, and joyfully.

In the liturgy we come together in the unity of the Holy Spirit as a priestly people. The baptized offer themselves as a spiritual sacrifice, while bishops and priests act in the Person of Christ, the head of the Church (235).

A Rich and Beautiful Tradition

We are familiar with the use of water, bread, wine, and oil as sacramental signs and symbols. We are also accustomed to gestures such as the laying on of hands. Some of these signs are drawn from nature. Others are drawn from human culture. All sacramental signs emerged in salvation history and were taken up by Christ to convey his saving truth and love. These signs are inseparable from the words that bear their meaning and power (*Compendium*, 236–238).

The liturgy by which we share in God's saving truth and love is to be celebrated, when possible, with music and song that beautifully express the Church's faith in a manner that lifts our minds and hearts to God. So too, the liturgy is celebrated in the presence of holy images, and above all the image of Christ. Images of the Blessed Virgin Mary, the saints, and the angels remind us that they are praying with us and for us in the liturgy of heaven (*Compendium*, 239–240).

If it is fitting that the liturgy be celebrated amid beautiful music, song, and images, it is also proper that it be celebrated in sacred buildings dedicated to the worship of God. When a church is consecrated, we see clearly the sacred importance of church furnishings: the altar, the pulpit, the tabernacle, the celebrant's chair, the baptismal font, and the confessional (*Compendium*, 244–246).

Indeed, the liturgy is very rich and beautiful. It has been celebrated for nearly two thousand years in a variety of languages and cultures (*Compendium*, 247). Amid such rich diversity, there is a oneness—thanks to apostolic tradition—in faith and sacramental life received from the apostles and handed down through the centuries. It is because the Church is catholic that she can welcome into her unity "all the authentic riches of cultures" while safeguarding what God has instituted for our salvation (248). The Church carefully distinguishes between those things in the liturgy that are unchangeable and those that can be rightfully adapted to human cultures throughout the world (249).

For Personal Reflection and Group Discussion

1. How do the sacraments make God's transforming grace present in the Church?

2. Why can the Sacraments of Baptism, Confirmation, and Holy Orders only be received once? How do you experience being "configured" to Christ?

3. How can we approach the sacraments with greater faith? How do you experience being nourished and strengthened at Mass and in Confession?

_____

_____

_____

_____

_____

4. What is the value and purpose of "sacramental signs" or symbols? What sacramental signs help you in your journey of faith?

_____

_____

_____

_____

_____

5. The liturgy (the public prayer of the Church) reflects both unity and diversity. Have you ever been part of a liturgical celebration in a different country or language? How was it the same? How was it different?

_____

_____

_____

_____

_____

22. Born Anew and Strengthened in Faith

THE SACRAMENTS OF BAPTISM AND CONFIRMATION
ALLOW US TO SHARE IN THE LIFE OF THE TRINITY

Compendium: 250–270
Scripture Passages: Romans 6:3-4; Titus 3:4-6

As a young priest, I routinely baptized many babies. When I asked their parents, "What do you desire for your children," they routinely answered, "Baptism." Only later did I begin to reflect on the significance of the question and the answer. The Church meant neither to be a mere formality. The underlying meaning of the question is "What is the deepest desire for your children?" And the meaning underlying the answer is "We want our children to be born anew, with that new life which Christ has won for us and that love which is stronger than sin and more powerful than death." Jesus' baptism—recorded in the Gospels (Matthew 3:13-17; Mark 1:9-11; Luke 3:21-22)—reminds us that, in the course of his public ministry, the Lord gave the Church her sacramental life.

When asked how we become members of the Church, most of us rightly answer, "Baptism." Yet our answer would not be complete if we omitted the other two sacraments of initiation. We who are "born anew in Baptism are strengthened by Confirmation and are then nourished by the Eucharist" (*Compendium*, 251).

Baptized into Christ

The word "baptize" means to immerse in water. Whether Baptism is carried out through immersion or, more commonly, through the pouring of water, the effect is the same: the newly baptized person is immersed in the death and resurrection of Christ. In Baptism we receive an initial sharing of the Holy Spirit and the theological virtues of faith, hope, and charity (*Compendium*, 252).

In God's plan of salvation, events such as Noah's building of the ark and the miraculous passage of the chosen people through the Red Sea were like a "forecast" or a "prefiguring" of Baptism. The story of Noah shows how water is both a source of death and of life, just as in Baptism, sin and death are "drowned" even as a new life of grace is engendered. In passing through the Red Sea, Israel was freed from slavery to Egypt. So too, when we pass through the waters of Baptism, we are freed from the slavery of sin. In crossing the Jordan, Israel inherited the Promised Land, an image of the eternal life that takes root in us (*Compendium*, 253). All of this was fulfilled in Christ.

To echo again the thought of St. Leo the Great, Christ's passage from death to life "passed over" into Baptism. Accordingly, the risen Christ sent the apostles out to preach the gospel and to baptize "all nations" in the name of the Trinity from the day of Pentecost onward (Matthew 28:19; *Compendium*, 254–255).

Who, then, can be baptized? The short answer is anyone not yet baptized (*Compendium*, 257). This includes infants, who are born with original sin (278). Through Baptism they are freed from the power of Satan and become children of God. When infants are baptized, their parents make a profession of faith for them. After attaining the use of reason, the baptized child makes his or her own profession of faith. The godparents and the whole Church, however, share in the responsibility of attracting people to the faith, helping them to prepare for Baptism (in the catechumenate) and to grow in the new life of faith and grace (258–259).

Many Catholics are baptized as infants. Parishes rightfully ask parents and godparents to undergo preparation for the Baptism of their children so that they will be better equipped to form their children in the Church's faith by word and example. Adults undergo formation for Baptism through what is known as the Rite of Christian Initiation of Adults, or simply the RCIA. This is more than receiving instruction in the faith. Rather, "the rite of Christian initiation presented here is designed for adults who, after hearing the mystery of Christ proclaimed, consciously and freely seek the living God and enter the way of faith and conversion as the Holy Spirit opens their hearts" (RCIA, Introduction, 1). Here it is well to remember that "Baptism, the Eucharist, and the sacrament of Confirmation together constitute the 'sacraments of Christian initiation,' whose unity must be safeguarded" (CCC, 1285).

Normally in the Latin Church, the bishop, priest or deacon administers the Sacrament of Baptism. In case of necessity, anyone can do so, provided that he or she "has the intention of doing what the Church does" and employs the correct form of the sacrament (*Compendium*, 260). Such latitude regarding the minister of Baptism is due to its importance. The words of the *Compendium* are instructive: "Baptism is necessary for salvation for all those to whom the Gospel has been proclaimed and who have had the possibility of asking for this sacrament" (261). In the strength of Christ's salvific will, however, others are saved without ordinary Baptism, including those who die for the faith (Baptism of blood); those who wish for the sacrament but cannot receive it, or those who, moved by grace, sincerely seek God (Baptism of desire). Children who die without Baptism are also entrusted to the mercy of God (262).

We should be grateful for the gift of our baptism, particularly when we reflect on its effects. It not only removes original sin but also takes away any sins committed prior to Baptism. Through the sacrament, we share in the life of the Trinity. This is called "sanctifying grace," and it joins us to Christ and makes us members of his body, the Church. Baptism also gives us a share in Christ's priesthood. United to his self-offering and freed from sin, we are enabled to offer up every aspect of our lives to God (*Compendium*, 263).

Confirmed by the Holy Spirit

The second sacrament of initiation, given to those already baptized, "is called *Confirmation* because it confirms and strengthens baptismal grace." In the Eastern churches it is called "Chrismation" to describe the heart of the rite itself—anointing with holy oil or chrism, blessed by the bishop on Holy Thursday (*Compendium*, 266). Like Baptism, Confirmation can be received only once (269). In the West, the bishop normally administers the sacrament, although he can delegate a priest to do so. In the East, priests ordinarily confer Chrismation immediately after Baptism (270).

This sacrament has deep roots in Scripture and tradition. The Old Testament prophets were anointed by the Holy Spirit. Not only was Jesus conceived by the power of the Holy Spirit, but he also lived his entire life and conducted his whole ministry in complete oneness with the Holy Spirit. At Pentecost the Holy Spirit came upon the apostles and enabled them to proclaim the teaching and saving deeds of Christ with courage and power. The apostles imparted the gift of the Holy Spirit to the newly baptized by the laying on of hands. Bishops, who are successors to the apostles, continue to do so in the Sacrament of Confirmation (*Compendium*, 267).

In a sense, Confirmation enables the recipient to share in the mystery of Pentecost. It brings about a special outpouring of the Holy Spirit in whom we are "sealed." We are permanently marked both as followers of Christ and as full members of the Church. Through this sacrament, the gifts of the Holy Spirit (wisdom, understanding, right judgment, courage, knowledge, reverence, and wonder and awe) are deepened in us. Thus, we are now more able to bear witness to Christ (*Compendium*, 268). Christian initiation is only complete with the reception of the Holy Eucharist. The Eucharist will be considered in the next chapter.

For Personal Reflection and Group Discussion

1. Why is Baptism so important? How would you share with someone who is not baptized what the sacrament means to you?

   _____

   _____

   _____

   _____

   _____

2. What does the baptized person receive through the Sacrament
   of Baptism? How have you seen these effects in your life? In the
   lives of others?

   _____

   _____

   _____

   _____

   _____

3. Reflect on some of the ways that the Old Testament "prefigures"
   the Sacrament of Baptism. Discuss how these Old Testament
   events and symbols relate to and point to Baptism.

   _____

   _____

   _____

   _____

   _____

4. Why is the second sacrament of initiation called "Confirmation"? How do the effects of this sacrament unfold over the course of our lives? How has it unfolded in your own life?

_____

_____

_____

_____

_____

5. What gifts of the Holy Spirit have impacted your life? Describe how you have concretely experienced or recognized at least one of the gifts of the Spirit empowering and/or strengthening you.

_____

_____

_____

_____

_____

23. Loving the Eucharist

*WE MUST GROW IN UNDERSTANDING OF AND REVERENCE FOR
THE GIFT OF THE HOLY EUCHARIST*

Compendium: 271–294
Scripture Passage: 1 Corinthians 11:23-26

Not long ago, a parishioner said to me that she just didn't see the need to go to Mass every Sunday. "I go to Mass once in a while, when I think it will help me," she said. Unfortunately, many people who consider themselves faithful Catholics share this attitude, an attitude that is not proportionate to the gift and mystery of the Eucharist. Yet once the gospel has found a place in our hearts and we have truly allowed ourselves to encounter Christ, then we begin to look at the Mass quite differently. No longer is it merely a ritual that might help or inspire me. It is where and how Christ is encountered in a deeply personal and real way. It is where his love can make deeper inroads into my life. It is how I can grow in discipleship in the community of the Church. It is where I can best express my love for the Lord in an act of perfect praise.

The *Compendium* offers a brief summary of this great mystery of faith: "The Eucharist is the very sacrifice of the Body and Blood of the Lord Jesus"(271). It is not merely a reminder that Christ offered his Body and Blood for our sake; rather, it is that offering. Jesus himself instituted the Eucharist "to perpetuate the sacrifice of the cross throughout the ages until his return in glory" (271). The Eucharist, the heart of the Church's life, is the banquet and living memorial of Christ's sacrifice. When we worthily partake of the Eucharist, we participate even now in God's own life.

Thanksgiving and Communion

Gathered with his apostles, Jesus entrusted the Eucharist to the Church at the Last Supper. At every Mass, the priest repeats and reenacts the words by which the Lord instituted the Eucharist: "Take this and eat it, all of you; this is my Body which will be given up for you. . . . Take this and drink of this, all of you. This is the cup of my Blood, the Blood of the new and everlasting covenant. It will be shed for you and for all so that sins may be forgiven. Do this in memory of me" (*Compendium*, 273).

We hear these words so often, but do we realize their significance?

Since the Eucharist re-presents (makes present again) the death and resurrection of Christ, it contains the entire spiritual wealth of the Church. It brings us into union (communion) with the Trinity and with one another. It puts us in touch with the great liturgy of heaven, that utterly joyous and eternal worship of God for which we were made and for which our hearts long (*Compendium*, 274, 287).

The more we think about what the Eucharist actually is, the less "optional" it seems! The very names used to describe the Eucharist remind us of its centrality. For example, the word "Eucharist" refers to the thanksgiving we owe to God. The phrase "Holy Mass" speaks to our mission to bring Christ into our daily lives. The Scriptures refer to the Eucharist as the "breaking of the bread"—a sharing in the Body of the Lord that makes us one. Finally, "Holy Communion" tells us that the Eucharist unites us to the Trinity, to the saints and angels in heaven, and to one another in the Church here on earth (*Compendium*, 275).

The Eucharist is at the very heart of the priesthood. Only a validly ordained priest or bishop who acts in the Person of Christ and in the name of the Church can offer the Eucharist (*Compendium*, 278). Through ordination, the priest is conformed to Christ—the great high priest—so that he can reenact Christ's words and deeds.

We also should not forget that the Eucharist was prefigured in the Passover. When Jesus gathered with his apostles in the upper room, they celebrated a Passover meal that commemorated the deliverance of the people of Israel from the slavery of Egypt to the freedom of the Promised Land. This deliverance foreshadowed the great deliverance we experience at the Eucharist: from the slavery of sin to the freedom of the new life of grace that Christ has won for us.

The Real Presence

Each time the Eucharist is celebrated, Jesus' sacrifice is truly made present: "The sacrifice of the cross and the sacrifice of the Eucharist are *one and the same sacrifice*" (*Compendium*, 280). Christ is both the priest and the victim. While his sacrifice on the cross occurred in a bloody manner, the Eucharist is offered in an unbloody manner, through the signs of bread and wine (280).

Jesus makes his sacrifice of love available to us so that we can offer our lives—our joys, our sorrows, and our daily work—in union with him to the Father as an acceptable sacrifice of praise. It is the most perfect prayer that we can offer for our loved ones and for all the living and the dead.

We can understand our need for the Eucharist by focusing on how Christ is present "in a true, real and substantial way, with his Body and his Blood, with his Soul and his Divinity" (*Compendium*, 282). Indeed, the Church has coined a word to describe the complete transformation of bread and wine into Christ's Body and Blood: "transubstantiation" (283).

This leads us to reflect on the respect we owe the Eucharistic species, the bread and wine transformed into Christ's Body and Blood. Christ is present whole and entirely in each particle of the Host and in each drop of the Precious Blood. The Eucharistic species should therefore be treated with reverence and great care. Since Christ is truly and substantially present, we worship the Eucharist both during Mass and outside of Mass.

Given the beauty and centrality of this sublime gift, the Church rightly obliges us to take part in Mass each Sunday (*Compendium*, 289). While we are obliged to receive Communion at least once a year, during the Easter season, the Church encourages frequent reception (290). To receive worthily, we must be members of the Catholic Church and be in the state of grace (291). If we are aware of any mortal sins we have committed, we should first receive the Sacrament of Penance. We should also prepare our hearts to receive our Lord in the Eucharist by prayerful recollection and by fasting one hour before Mass. Finally, we should show respect for the Eucharist by our prayerful demeanor and by dressing appropriately when attending Mass. In each of these ways, let us embrace in love this great mystery of faith.

For Personal Reflection and Group Discussion

1. How do Jesus' words and actions at the Last Supper deepen your understanding of his sacrifice for us and the price he paid for our redemption?

2. In what sense is the Eucharist a meal of fellowship? An *agape* (love) feast? A sacrificial meal? A thanksgiving banquet?

3. Share about how receiving Christ's Body and Blood sacramentally has transformed you and/or borne fruit in your life.

_____

_____

_____

_____

_____

4. What is your attitude toward the Eucharist? How (well) do you prepare yourself to participate at Mass and receive Communion in a meaningful and reverent way?

_____

_____

_____

_____

_____

5. If your participation at Mass has become routine or if you feel bored at Mass, what might you do to renew your appreciation of it or increase your attentiveness?

_____

_____

_____

_____

24. The Sacraments of Healing

THROUGH THE SACRAMENTS OF PENANCE AND THE ANOINTING OF THE SICK, THE CHURCH CONTINUES CHRIST'S HEALING MINISTRY

Compendium: 295–320
Scripture Passage: James 5:14-15

When he walked the earth, Jesus forgave sins and healed those who were ill. He often linked the forgiveness of sins and physical healing, as in the case of the paralytic whose cure is recounted in the second chapter of Mark's Gospel. At other times, Jesus' forgiveness was not linked to a physical cure. In the eighth chapter of John's Gospel, for example, we read how Jesus forgave a woman caught in adultery. Because he forgives sin and heals sickness, we rightly call Jesus the "Divine Physician." Rejoicing and giving thanks, the Church continues the Lord's work of forgiving and healing through the Sacraments of Reconciliation and the Anointing of the Sick (*Compendium*, 295).

Seeking Forgiveness

The Sacrament of Penance is indeed the sacrament of God's mercy. I have experienced this often as a penitent and also as a confessor. It is a moment when God's healing love is applied to the spiritual wounds of our lives. It is a moment when we can experience God's love as stronger than our sins. It is a moment of freedom and joy.

The Sacrament of Penance goes by several names: Reconciliation, Confession, or the Sacrament of Forgiveness or Conversion. These names highlight various aspects of the sacrament: it reconciles us to God and to the Church; it brings us God's forgiveness; it is how we acknowledge our sins and repent; and it is a powerful means of conversion (*Compendium*, 296).

The experience of our sinfulness and fragility readily illustrates why the Lord gave us this sacrament on that first Easter evening (*Compendium*, 298). Although Baptism gives us a new life of grace, a tendency toward sin, called "concupiscence," remains as a result of the fall. Mortal sin separates us from God and damages our relationship with the Church. And venial sin, while not destroying our friendship with God, weakens our relationship with him and others. Through the Church and her ministry of reconciliation, Christ's call to lifelong conversion is addressed to the baptized (297, 299).

Although the season of Lent focuses on the need for repentance, our daily lives should always be marked by genuine sorrow for our sins. We manifest a contrite and humble heart (Psalm 51:19) when we fast, pray, and give to those in need.

If we commit a mortal sin, we are obliged to go to Confession before receiving Holy Communion (*Compendium*, 305). Strictly speaking, we are not obliged to confess venial sins. Nonetheless, we should regularly confess even our venial sins—which is sometimes called "devotional Confession"—in order to resist temptation and grow in virtue (306).

Sometimes people hesitate to go to Confession because they have forgotten how to do so. There are several things that we, as penitents, must do: make a careful examination of conscience based on the Ten Commandments and the Beatitudes; make a sincere Act of Contrition; confess our sins to a priest—all mortal sins not yet confessed as well as venial sins; and fulfill the acts of penance that the confessor assigns to us (*Compendium*, 303–304). Note that contrition is perfect when it is motivated only by love of God; it is imperfect if fear of just punishment is the motivation. Contrition also includes a firm resolve not to sin again and to avoid the near occasions of sin.

Since Christ entrusted the power to forgive sins to the apostles and their successors, only a bishop or priest can hear confessions. Bishops and priests act in the Person of Christ through the power of the Holy Spirit to grant the Father's forgiveness (*Compendium*,

307). Bound to absolute secrecy, they listen attentively and help penitents open their hearts to the Lord's mercy, amend their lives, and grow in discipleship (309). A confessor can offer general absolution only "in cases of serious necessity," such as impending death or some grave emergency (311).

As the Sacrament of Penance brings about the forgiveness of our sins, we are reconciled with God and the Church. The eternal punishment due to mortal sin is remitted, and some of the temporal punishment due to sin is taken away. Temporal punishment is further remitted through prayers and good works, to which indulgences are attached (*Compendium*, 312). This sacrament also brings us peace, serenity, joy, and strength for living the gospel.

Healing the Sick

As a priest, I have often been privileged to be at the bedside of the sick and dying. If our need for the Lord can get obscured in the rough and tumble of life, it often clearly emerges amid suffering, whether a chronic illness or a life-threatening injury or illness. What a beautiful gift is the second sacrament of healing, the Anointing of the Sick! As he healed the sick, Jesus showed that he was ushering in the kingdom of God and its victory over sin, suffering, and death.

The Church continues the Lord's compassionate care for the sick and dying in many ways. In many parts of the world, through its hospitals and clinics, the Church is the largest provider of medical services. Through the Anointing of the Sick, celebrated only by a bishop or a priest, the Church ministers in the Lord's name to those in danger of death or those who begin "to be in danger of death because of sickness or old age" (*Compendium*, 316). In the Latin rite, this sacrament is celebrated by anointing the sick person with oil on the forehead and hands. In all cases, a prayer accompanies the anointing (James 5:14-15; *Compendium*, 318). If possible, the person suffering from serious illness should go to Confession prior to being anointed.

The Sacrament of Anointing unites the sick person more closely to the suffering, death, and resurrection of Christ and contributes to the salvation of the patient and to the good of the whole Church. This sacrament also provides comfort, consolation, serenity, and courage to patients in their suffering. If the sick person is unable to go to Confession, this sacrament brings about the forgiveness of sins. If it is God's will, it can also restore a sick person to health. In every case, this sacrament prepares the recipient for everlasting life (*Compendium*, 319).

As we thank God for the gift of these two sacraments, may we pray for our own conversion and for the conversion of sinners everywhere. May we also pray for those who are seriously ill, especially those who have asked for our prayers.

For Personal Reflection and Group Discussion

1. Discuss the significance of the various names by which the Sacrament of Reconciliation is known. What are the primary effects of this sacrament?

_____

_____

_____

_____

_____

2. What is your attitude toward going to Confession? Is it difficult for you to believe that God loves you in spite of your failings and forgives your sins?

_____

_____

_____

_____

_____

3. Recall an occasion when you received Christ's forgiveness for
   your sins. In what way did this forgiveness set you free? Offer
   a silent prayer of thanksgiving to the Lord for how he show-
   ered his love, mercy, and grace on you through the Sacrament of
   Reconciliation.

   _____

   _____

   _____

   _____

   _____

4. What are the effects and benefits of the Sacrament of the Anointing of the Sick? If you have ever received this sacrament, what
   benefit did you experience?

   _____

   _____

   _____

   _____

   _____

5. In what ways does your parish minister to and offer help to the sick? If possible, this week visit someone (for example, a family member or relative, neighbor, fellow parishioner, or co-worker) who is ill and in need of consolation, encouragement, prayer support, and/or practical assistance.

_____

_____

_____

_____

_____

25. Sacraments of Vocation

Through Holy Orders and Matrimony, Christians Are Given Special Graces and a Particular Mission

Compendium: 321–353
Scripture Passages: Hebrews 7:26-28; Matthew 19:4-6

In Baptism we receive a vocation to love—to love God above all and to love our neighbor not only as we love ourselves, but indeed as God loves us. As we come to follow Christ more fully and enter more robustly into the life of the Church, the Holy Spirit helps us discern what specific form our baptismal call to love should take, including a vocation to the ordained ministry and holy matrimony. These vocations are rooted in two sacraments, Holy Orders and Matrimony. They are called sacraments of "communion and mission" because they equip married couples and the ordained for their missions of service in building up the Church (*Compendium*, 321).

Three Degrees

Christ instituted the Sacrament of Holy Orders to continue his saving work. Bishops, priests, and deacons are "ordained to exercise a *sacred power* in the name and with the authority of Christ" to the sanctification of others (*Compendium*, 323).

The Book of Genesis mentions the royal priesthood of Melchizedek, whose priesthood was not inherited but was given directly from God. His offering clearly foreshadowed the priesthood of Christ (Hebrews 7), who is God's only begotten Son. Jesus, the "one mediator" between God and men, offered himself in obedient love on the cross to reconcile sinners to God (1 Timothy 2:5). This is the heart of his priesthood, and the ministerial priesthood is, in turn, a sacramental sharing of Christ's gift (*Compendium*, 324).

Holy Orders has three ranks or degrees: the episcopate (bishop), the presbyterate (priest), and the diaconate (deacon) (*Compendium*, 325). The bishop shares the fullness of the priesthood and is a successor to the apostles. He is part of the college of bishops united under the pope in caring for particular churches (dioceses), with the offices of teaching, sanctifying, and ruling (326).

Priests are the bishops' closest co-workers. Through ordination, the Holy Spirit transforms the priest by indelibly fashioning in his soul the image of Christ, head and shepherd of the Church. Thus empowered to act in the very Person of Christ and in the name of the Church, the priest re-presents the Lord's saving deeds (*Compendium*, 336). He does this by preaching the gospel and celebrating the sacraments—especially the Eucharist.

Deacons are "configured to Christ the servant of all," who came "not to be served but to serve" (*Compendium*, 330; Matthew 20:28). They are charged with preaching the word, assisting at the altar and in the Church's sacramental life, and serving those in need. Those preparing for priestly ordination are called "transitional deacons" while others are called "permanent deacons."

Only bishops can validly confer the Sacrament of Holy Orders. The bishop lays his hands on the head of those to be ordained and prays the solemn prayer of consecration, asking the Holy Spirit to pour out his gifts (*Compendium*, 331–332).

In the Latin (Western) Church, priests are called to celibacy "for the sake of the kingdom of heaven" (Matthew 19:12). Married men are eligible to become permanent deacons. In the Eastern churches, married men may become priests, but marriage is not permitted after one has been ordained. In both East and West, bishops are always chosen from among celibate priests (*Compendium*, 334).

Christ gave the gift of Holy Orders to his Church in order to hand on his saving word and to continue his work of healing and sanctifying. Bishops, priests, and deacons are to model their lives on Christ, pray deeply, and live the gospel fully so that, being missionary disciples themselves, they may set people's hearts on fire with God's love and lead them by word and Sacrament deep into the heart of Christ. As we reflect on this sacrament, let us pray for an increase of vocations to the priesthood and the diaconate.

Faithful, Fruitful Love

We turn now to the Sacrament of Matrimony, which is critically important for both the Church and society. The marriage of a man and woman is fundamental in God's plan of creation and redemption. It is an institution older than all organized religion and is part of every civilization.

Created in the divine image, male and female are different yet complementary—made for each other. This unity-in-difference is at the heart of marriage. In God's plan, marriage exists both for the union and good of the spouses and for the procreation and education of children.

From the beginning, God's plan for marriage was disrupted by sin. Throughout history, marriage has been affected by conflict and infidelity (*Compendium*, 339). In our time, it is threatened by the widespread practice of divorce, contraception, and current legislative efforts for same-sex marriage.

God has sought not only to repair the damage of sin, but also to make marriage the sign of his love. The Old Testament taught that God's covenant with Israel was nuptial—a marriage of God and his people. That nuptial covenant foreshadowed the new covenant of Christ and his bride, the Church (Ephesians 5:25). Christian marriage is modeled on the Lord's love for his people, a love that is faithful, permanent, and fruitful. These are the same characteristics that are fundamental to the marriage relationship and the sacrificial love that is at the heart of it (*Compendium*, 340–341). Spouses, united to Christ and to the Church, are called and given the grace to form a family that is a community of faith, prayer, and virtue.

The Sacrament of Matrimony is normally celebrated before a priest or deacon. Matrimonial consent is given when a man and a woman willingly give themselves to each other irrevocably in order to live a covenant of faithful and fruitful love (*Compendium*, 344). For the sacrament to be valid, this consent must be given freely and consciously. A valid marriage that is ratified and consummated can never be dissolved.

A marriage between a Catholic and a baptized non-Catholic is called a "mixed marriage." A marriage between a Catholic and a non-Christian is called "disparity of cult," and a dispensation is required for validity. In both cases, the non-Catholic party is advised of the obligation of the Catholic to see that their children will be baptized and formed in the faith of the Church (*Compendium*, 345).

Recognizing the challenges that married couples face, the Church seeks to help them remain faithful. Sadly, this sometimes proves all but impossible. Pope Francis has asked the Church to reflect prayerfully on the ways in which the Church can best assist couples who find themselves in this difficult situation. The practice of the Church, deeply rooted in the Lord's own teaching, is that after a divorce, neither spouse is free to marry again unless the previous marriage has been declared null by the Church authority. Those who are divorced and remarried without an annulment cannot receive sacramental absolution or Holy Communion. Nonetheless, the Church must listen and attend to people in this situation; those in pastoral ministry are to assist them in staying close to the Church, in finding the support they need, and in helping them lead a life of faith, prayer, generosity towards those in need, and closeness to their children (*Compendium*, 349).

Finally, those called to the consecrated life or priestly celibacy do not belittle marriage by renouncing it. Indeed, like married couples they spiritually participate in Christ's spousal relationship of love with his Church. Priests are truly to be wise and loving spiritual fathers whose pastoral service bears abundant fruit. Those in consecrated lives are to manifest by evangelical counsels the marriage of the human soul to Christ. Further, they are "a sign of the absolute supremacy of Christ's love and of the ardent expectation of his glorious return" as we look to the wedding feast of heaven (*Compendium*, 342).

For Personal Reflection and Group Discussion

1. Have you ever thought of the Sacraments of Matrimony and Holy Orders as sacraments of communion and mission? How might this change the way you view them?

2. What are the primary tasks a priest carries out in his priestly ministry? How does the ministerial priesthood of the Church reflect Christ's priesthood?

3. Why is marriage critically important for the Church and for society? How might you communicate that to someone who is cohabitating?

_____

_____

_____

_____

_____

4. Explain and discuss the importance of male and female complementarity and the "unity-in-difference" that is at the heart of marriage. How do you see this played out in your own marriage or in marriages of other couples?

_____

_____

_____

_____

_____

5. What do the consecrated life and priestly celibacy say to the world today? Why is that important?

_____

_____

_____

_____

_____

26. Morality, Freedom, and Human Dignity

CHRISTIAN LIFE AND MORALITY LEAD TO, RATHER THAN TAKE AWAY FROM, TRUE FREEDOM AND HAPPINESS

Compendium: 357–369
Scripture Passage: Matthew 5:1-11

The *Compendium* helps us to see how all the parts of our faith fit together. As we turn to the third pillar of the *Catechism*, dedicated to the Church's moral teaching, it is important to recall that it is through the grace of the Holy Spirit at work in the Church's belief and worship that we are enabled to live as God's children and true followers of Christ (*Compendium*, 357).

Yet many people—even active members of the Church—tend to think of morality merely as "rules." They fail to see that morality has to do with our human dignity and happiness. We are made in God's image and likeness; more than complex animals, we are endowed not only with a body, but also with an immortal soul, as well as intelligence and free will (*Compendium*, 358). What is more, we are called by God to be formed and shaped by his truth and love so that we may one day share his life forever in heaven.

The Freedom to Love

Sad to say, many people look for happiness in the wrong places, such as in the quest for money, power, or illicit pleasures. The Church, on the other hand, urges us to look for happiness in an unlikely place: the eight Beatitudes. To be sure, Jesus' teachings on being poor in spirit, pure of heart, and meek and humble do not sound like a recipe for fun—but they *are* the path to peace and joy. The Beatitudes are the self-portrait of Jesus, who demonstrates what it means to be fully human (*Gaudium et Spes*, 22). They do not represent an impossible ideal or an extra set of commandments but show us the kind of people we can become if we live the teachings of Christ. This way of life enlarges our capacity to receive God's love so that we can love God above all things and our neighbors as ourselves (*Compendium*, 362). By embracing the truth, receiving the graces offered by the sacraments, and acting in charity, we grow in intimacy with God.

It is in choosing what is good in daily life that we respond to God's love for us and, at the same time, shape and determine what sort of people we will become (St. John Paul II, *Veritatis Splendor* [The Splendor of Truth], 65). Christian morality is a way of life in which we are transformed into unique living images of Jesus and vital members of his body, the Church. Our human dignity is linked to God's utterly generous call to share in his life and love, a supernatural calling that exceeds our human capacities. Embedded in each of our moral choices is an implicit decision for or against God and his love (*Compendium*, 362).

Freedom is an essential part of human dignity. We cannot really love God and neighbor unless we do so freely. Human freedom is God-given; it is not granted by any earthly authority. It enables us to make choices and to take responsibility. We can easily choose the wrong path, but this actually diminishes our freedom and leads us into moral slavery. Think, for example, of those enslaved by drugs, alcohol, or sex. On the contrary, the more we choose what is good, the freer we become to love (*Compendium*, 363).

Choosing Good or Evil

Although contemporary culture touts freedom, it is less enthusiastic in speaking about responsibility. Yet freedom and responsibility go hand in hand. To the extent that an action is truly voluntary, we are responsible for it. Sometimes our responsibility is diminished by factors beyond our control, such as ignorance or deeply ingrained habits (*Compendium*, 364). Though flawed and limited, freedom is essential to human dignity. Civil authority must respect human freedom, "especially in moral and religious matters," with due regard for "the common good and a just public order" (365).

Human freedom, the Church teaches, was gravely damaged because of original sin but not totally destroyed. It has been further weakened by countless personal sins. Christ came to free us from sin so that, through the grace of the Holy Spirit, we can freely choose the good and become his disciples in building up the Church and contributing to a just and peaceful society.

But what makes an action morally good? Today people often think that it is up to them to decide what is right or wrong. By contrast, the *Compendium* teaches that the morality of a human act has three sources. First, the *object* of a moral choice may be truly good or something that is objectively evil. Some things, such as the killing of an innocent person, must never be chosen because they are evil in and of themselves. Second, the *intention* of the one who acts must be taken into account. A person may choose the good for either a good or a bad reason. Conversely, a good intention does not make a bad choice good; the ends do not justify the means. Often our moral choices have more than one intention; it is important to prudently sort them out in accord with the Church's time-tested wisdom so that we may choose what is right and good even in life's complex situations. Third, the *circumstances* surrounding an action (including its consequences) increase or diminish one's moral responsibility—but again, this cannot make an objectively bad choice good. For a human act to be morally good, all three things must be aligned: something objectively good must be chosen for good reasons given the circumstances (*Compendium*, 367–369).

Let us rejoice that the risen Lord, through his Spirit, has set us free to choose what is truly good and life-giving!

For Personal Reflection and Group Discussion

1. Where do you seek happiness? How are the Beatitudes a way to happiness?

_____

_____

_____

_____

_____

2. What is the source of our freedom as human beings? What does human freedom enable us to do?

_____

_____

_____

_____

_____

3. What is the relationship and interplay between freedom and human dignity? Between freedom and responsibility? In what ways might you have abused your God-given freedom or shirked the responsibilities that are inherent to freedom?

_____

_____

_____

_____

4. On what three sources does the morality of a human act depend? What criteria are often used today to justify a moral act? What might be lacking in those cases?

_____

_____

_____

_____

_____

5. Have you ever been tempted by or succumbed to the faulty reasoning that "the end justifies the means" to excuse a poor or wrong moral choice that you have made? Why does the Church reject this rationale?

_____

_____

_____

_____

_____

27. Virtue and Vice

*A WELL-FORMED CONSCIENCE AND THE PRACTICE OF VIRTUE LEAD US
TOWARD HOLINESS AND AWAY FROM SIN*

Compendium: 370–400
Scripture Passage: Galatians 5:22-23

L et your conscience be your guide." Sometimes this phrase is taken to mean that our consciences create the truth about what is right or wrong—that is, what is right for me might be wrong for you, and vice versa. In reality, the conscience is at the very core of where God speaks to us. It is a judgment of reason that directs us to choose what is good and avoid what is evil. It does not establish moral truth but instead perceives it. This is how we take responsibility for our thoughts, words, and deeds (*Compendium*, 372).

A well-formed conscience listens to the voice of God. It pays attention to the natural law (that is, the inner sense of right and wrong etched by the Creator on the human heart; see Romans 2:15) and to the word of God conveyed by the Church. The gifts of the Holy Spirit, received in Baptism and deepened in us through Confirmation, help us know and do what is good and affirm our God-given dignity (*Compendium*, 374). In forming one's conscience, each person must carefully respect the rights of others and the good of society (373).

The conscience should follow three ground rules. First, we may never do evil so that good may result from it. Second, we should treat others as we wish to be treated. And third, we must respect others and their consciences while avoiding the trap of accepting as good that which is evil (*Compendium*, 375). We are right indeed to follow our consciences, but we can reach wrong judgments. We are culpable when we deliberately fail to see the wrongness of an action. Sometimes, in spite of our best efforts, we may reach a wrong decision (376).

Doing the Good

A well-formed conscience is strengthened by virtue. The *Compendium* defines virtue as a "habitual and firm disposition to do the good" (377). We are shaped by the decisions we make, and when we habitually choose what is good, we grow in the likeness of God.

The Church distinguishes two types of virtue: human and theological. Human virtues strengthen us to control our desires and to guide our conduct according to reason and faith. We acquire them by repeatedly doing what is good. God's grace purifies and elevates human virtues. They are grouped under the four cardinal virtues on which the entire moral life is hinged. These include *prudence*, which strengthens our reason so that we may discern not only the good to be done in a particular situation, but also the best way to do it. *Justice* strengthens the will so that we will give to others—and to God—what is their due. *Fortitude* makes us firm in choosing the good, even when it is difficult or costly to do so. And *temperance* helps us achieve self-mastery over our desires for pleasure and the use of this world's goods (*Compendium*, 377–383).

The theological virtues—faith, hope, and charity—are from God and direct us to God. Unlike human virtues, they are not acquired by practice but are infused in us through the Holy Spirit. These grow through prayer and through the Church's sacramental life. They strengthen our relationship with the Trinity and help us to follow Christ by living the law of love (*Compendium*, 384).

Faith enables us to believe in God, in all that he has revealed and in what the Church proposes for our belief. By faith we affirm that God is truth itself and commit ourselves freely to God. *Hope* enables us to live in the present, in expectation of eternal life. Through hope, we rely on the Holy Spirit to persevere and prepare for the joy of heaven. *Charity* enables us to love God above all things and our neighbor as ourselves. By sharing in God's love revealed in Christ, we find the strength to live the law of love (*Compendium*, 385–388).

The twelve fruits of the Holy Spirit are the signs that we are becoming more Christlike by living the law of love in the spirit of the Beatitudes. "The tradition of the Church lists twelve of them: charity, joy, peace, patience, kindness, goodness, generosity, gentleness, faithfulness, modesty, self-control, and chastity" (*Compendium*, 390; cf. Galatians 5:22-23).

Sin and Repentance

Since we are inclined to sin, it is often not easy to do the good. Sin is a thought, word, or action that offends against God's love. In sinning against God, we wound our human dignity and weaken both the Church and the wider community. By his suffering and death, Jesus revealed the seriousness of sin while overcoming it by his merciful love (*Compendium*, 392). We accept the mercy of God when in the light of God's truth and love, we admit our sins and allow his love to heal us (391).

Sin can be directed against God, one's neighbor, or oneself. There are sins of thought, word, and deed, as well as sins of omission (*Compendium*, 393). The distinction between mortal and venial sins is very important. Mortal sins involve grave matter, full knowledge, and full consent of the will. They deprive us of sanctifying grace. If we fail to repent of them, we risk losing eternal life. Baptism and the Sacrament of Penance are the ordinary ways they are forgiven (395). Venial sins weaken our relationship with God and others. They impede us from progress in virtue and in the spiritual life. We should seek forgiveness of venial sins in the Sacrament of Penance and mortify ourselves so as to be purified from the effects of all the sins we have committed.

Sin can take hold of us when it is repeated. Habitual sins are called vices. These cloud the conscience and incline us toward evil. The main vices correspond to the capital sins: pride, avarice, envy, anger, lust, gluttony, and sloth. We must also be on guard not to cooperate with the sins of others. Finally, it is important to recognize that human sinfulness has given rise to social structures that are contrary to God's truth and love (398–400).

For Personal Reflection and Group Discussion

1. How is a moral conscience formed to be truthful and upright? What ground rules or norms should be followed by a moral conscience?

_____

_____

_____

_____

_____

2. What are the human virtues? What evidence or effects of the human, or cardinal, virtues do you recognize in your own life?

_____

_____

_____

_____

_____

3. What is the origin and source of the theological virtues? How can these virtues be strengthened in one's life? Discuss the impact of the theological virtues on you personally.

_____

_____

_____

_____

_____

4. How are the fruits of the Holy Spirit (Galatians 5:22-23) formed in us? Which of these fruits do you experience being manifested in your life?

_____

_____

_____

_____

_____

5. What is sin? How does sin affect human nature and human solidarity? How are sins distinguished according to their seriousness and gravity?

_____

_____

_____

_____

_____

28. The Human Community

Compendium: 401–414
Scripture Passage: 1 Peter 2:13-17

It is often said that the Church should stay out of politics. And indeed, the Church should refrain from partisan politics—explicitly favoring one candidate or party over another. In another sense, the Church must remain in politics—that is, the principled quest for a just and humane society that serves the common good. This is because ultimately, we can only find happiness in community, in association with other persons endowed by God with life and dignity and called to friendship with him. In truth, the one God is a community of Persons: Father, Son, and Holy Spirit. Since we are made in God's image and since Christ in some way has united himself to each person, human fraternity is modeled to some extent on the oneness of the Holy Trinity. Here we find the ultimate basis for the link between love of God and love of neighbor (*Compendium*, 401).

The Rule of Law

In countries like the United States, there are intense debates about the size and scope of government institutions and programs. These debates, however, are sure to go awry when we forget that "the human *person* is and ought to be the principle, the subject and the end of all social institutions" (*Compendium*, 402). In other words, social institutions should exist for the good of human beings—not the other way around. All human beings need social institutions, beginning with the family and extending to the local civic community and one's nation. We are also increasingly linked to the international community.

Over time, the Church took up and refined the principle of "sub-sidiarity" to protect the human person from being overwhelmed and harmed by large, faceless bureaucratic institutions and structures. The *Compendium* explains that "a community of a higher order should not assume the task belonging to a community of a lower order and deprive it of its authority" (403). The most basic human structure is the family, based on the marriage of a man and woman. It is in the interest of all, including the state, that family life be strong. And as a rule, the state should not preempt parental authority, as happens, for instance, when laws permit minors to procure abortions without parental notification. In a well-functioning society, institutions such as national and regional governments assist and support families and local governments so that they can function well.

Because of the reality of sin, human society will always be less than perfect and even deeply flawed. Nonetheless, the cause of human freedom must be won over in every age, and instead of becoming cynical, we must continue to seek what is authentically good for ourselves, our families, and our society. This means giving priority to "ethics over technology" and acknowledging "the primacy of the person over things" and "the superiority of spirit over matter" (St. John Paul II, *Redemptor Hominis*, 16). To retrieve these values and keep them from becoming lost, we stand in continual need of repentance, and the Church must often stand in the breach to call for changes in laws and social structures. Furthermore, as Pope Francis has said, "By her very nature the Church is missionary; she abounds in effective charity and a compassion which understands, assists and promotes" (*Evangelii Gaudium*, 179; cf. *Compendium*, 404).

The Common Good

Many people today tend to distrust or disrespect authority. Yet in God's plan, every human community, from the largest to the smallest, needs legitimate authority (*Compendium*, 405). Of course, authorities do make mistakes and sometimes break faith. The legitimate exercise of authority requires the personal integrity of leaders; it also requires that the common good be sought using morally licit means. The Church understands the common good as "the sum of those conditions of social life which allow social groups and their individual members relatively thorough and ready access to their own fulfillment" (*Gaudium et Spes*, 26). In seeking the common good, the dignity of each person, especially the most vulnerable, must always be respected. Laws that are unjust and immoral "are not binding in conscience" (*Compendium*, 406). Finally, governments are to be constituted and to function by the free decisions of citizens, and leaders should respect "the rule of law" rather than imposing their own will on others (406).

It is not only leaders of social institutions that have a responsibility to seek the common good; all of us must do so by living up to our vocations, by doing our work well, and by being loyal and engaged citizens. The common good is all those conditions that enable individuals and groups within society to flourish. It is best secured in communities that defend the dignity of individual citizens and promote various social institutions that truly assist citizens while calling them to seek the good of the nation and the world as a whole (*Compendium*, 407–410).

In such a society, where authority is exercised well and wisely, social justice is more likely ensured. In other words, society is better able to help individuals and groups attain what is their due, such as the freedom to speak freely in the public square and the opportunity to pursue beneficial goals (*Compendium*, 411).

The attainment of the common good and genuine social justice is based on human solidarity. We are bound together because all persons are created in God's image, are endowed with a rational soul, share the same nature, and are called by Christ to happiness in heaven (*Compendium*, 412, 414). Despite this fact, there is a growing disparity between the rich and poor, affecting millions of people. We cannot be complacent about these inequities, which are contrary to the gospel. Instead, we must work for a more just and humane society and practice generous charity. Indeed, the principles of charity, unity, fraternity, and patriotism track closely the Church's social teaching and call us to work for the common good of all.

For Personal Reflection and Group Discussion

1. Discuss why "a community of a higher order should not assume the task belonging to a community of a lower order and deprive it of its authority" (*Compendium*, 403). What are the reasons underlying this statement?

_____

_____

_____

_____

_____

2. In what ways do you see the state supporting parental authority? Preempting parental authority? Give some concrete examples of both.

_____

_____

_____

_____

_____

3. Do you recognize any situations in your personal life in which you are not acknowledging the "primacy of the person over things" (*Redemptor Hominis*, 16)?

_____

_____

_____

_____

_____

4. What does the legitimate exercise of authority require and promote? Have you ever had to stand up against an unjust or immoral law or the illicit exercise of authority?

_____

_____

_____

_____

_____

5. What is involved in the common good? Do you tend to be more motivated by self-interest and selfishness than by a concern for others? How are you actively seeking the common good, promoting a more humane society, and/or practicing generous charity?

_____

_____

_____

_____

_____

29. God's Salvation: Law and Grace

The Moral Law, Rooted in Divine Wisdom and Written on the Human Heart, Is Fulfilled in Our Life with Christ

Compendium: 415–433
Scripture Passage: Romans 2:15

When public figures defend a moral truth, they are likely to be accused of imposing their religious beliefs on others—as, for example, when a politician defends unborn human life from the evil of abortion. It is true that religious faith may clarify moral teachings and allow us to see their importance in this life and in the life to come. Nonetheless, many—if not most—moral teachings are accessible to human reason. How can this be? The answer lies in a correct understanding of the moral law.

As the *Compendium* explains, the moral law is not simply a set of human rules but "a work of divine Wisdom" that shows the way to true happiness and teaches us to shun those things that lead us away from God (415). St. Paul teaches that the demands of the moral law are written on the human heart by the Creator (Romans 2:15). This share in God's wisdom is called "natural law," which gives us an inherent sense of right and wrong and forms the basis for the rights and duties of individuals and communities (416).

The Old and New Law

Because of sin, not everyone clearly perceives the natural law. For this reason, St. Augustine said, God "wrote on the tables of the Law what men did not read in their hearts" (*Compendium*, 417). The Ten Commandments summarize the moral teaching of the Old Testament, also known as the "Old Law." In this context, "old" does not mean outmoded, useless, or no longer true. Rather, it means that the moral teaching of the Old Testament was the first stage of the revealed law, which in turn was completed and fulfilled by the gospel (418).

The Ten Commandments express moral truths known naturally by reason, thus verifying the natural law. In laying the foundations for the human vocation to love God and neighbor, they are "a privileged expression of the natural law" (CCC, 2070; cf. *Compendium*, 418). In teaching unchanging moral truth, they are also a "tutor" that prepared the way for the gospel. The Old Law, however, remains imperfect. While it teaches moral truth, it does not provide the strength of the Holy Spirit (419).

The "New Law," which can be found in the New Testament, especially in the Beatitudes, was both proclaimed and fulfilled by Christ (*Compendium*, 420–421). Here the word "new" does not indicate a rupture with the Old Law. Jesus said, "Do not think that I have come to abolish the law or the prophets. I have come not to abolish but to fulfill" (Matthew 5:17). The gospel is new because it originated in the Person of Christ, the incarnate Son of God, whose teaching, death, and resurrection fully revealed the Father's love. Through the Holy Spirit, believers share in Christ's risen life, are drawn into intimacy with the Father, and are enabled to love others as they are loved by Christ (420).

Indeed, Christ came to "justify" us in the power of the Holy Spirit. Justification is God's mercy at work to make us holy by granting us remission of our sins and a share in his goodness. We are justified by the grace of the Holy Spirit, which Christ won for us by his death and resurrection. God freely gives us grace, a share in his divine life that enables us to respond to his love and to live in his friendship. This is called "sanctifying" or "deifying" grace because it makes us participants in the life of the Trinity. This gift is supernatural because it cannot be learned or earned; it can only be received from God. Sanctifying grace is "habitual" because we are to remain in the state of grace throughout our lives (*Compendium*, 423).

In addition, there are "actual" graces that help us do God's will in the various circumstances of our lives. Each sacrament also confers a special grace on us (*Compendium*, 424). Ultimately, God's grace does not infringe on our human freedom but frees us to fulfill our deepest yearnings to share his life and love (425).

Called to Holiness

Although we cannot earn or merit eternal life, we can lead virtuous lives through God's grace. In other words, once we are in the state of grace, God freely grants us his reward for a life of virtue. We are to strive for virtue, not only for ourselves, but to strengthen the entire Church (*Compendium*, 426–427). All the baptized are called to holiness—that is, the fullness of love brought about through intimacy with Christ (428).

The Church helps us attain holiness by teaching the truth of Christ and leading us to share in his saving love through the sacraments. Filled with the grace of the Holy Spirit, we can come to see morality not as a grim duty but as a response of praise to the God of love. Among the Church's teachings are precepts that help us understand what it means to be a practicing Catholic. These include attending Mass on Sunday and holy days of obligation as well as refraining from work or other activities that might prevent us from worshipping on those days; confessing one's sins and receiving the Sacrament of Penance at least once each year; receiving Holy Communion at least once a year during the Easter season; observing the Church's discipline with regard to fasting and abstinence; and helping to provide for the material needs of the Church according to one's abilities (*Compendium*, 430–432).

When our lives reflect the truth, goodness, and beauty of Christ's love, people around us are drawn to the gospel and to the Person of Christ (*Compendium*, 433). Indeed, all of us are called both to holiness and to the work of evangelization.

For Personal Reflection and Group Discussion

1. Discuss your understanding of moral law and natural law.

2. What is the relationship between the natural law and the "Old Law," that is, the moral teachings of the Old Testament?

3. Why is the Old Law considered imperfect? What is the "New Law" or the "Law of the Gospel"?

4. What are the purposes and effects of sanctifying grace? Of actual graces? Share about a grace you received that helped you to do God's will, even if it was something difficult.

_____

_____

_____

_____

_____

5. What is your disposition toward the precepts of the Church? What might help you to overcome difficulties you might have in fulfilling these precepts? Do you offer a strong witness to others as a practicing Catholic?

_____

_____

_____

_____

_____

30. Loving God Above All

THE FIRST THREE COMMANDMENTS PERTAIN TO OUR DUTY
TO LOVE GOD WITH OUR ENTIRE BEING

Compendium: 434–454
Scripture Passages: Exodus 20:2-17; Matthew 19:16-19

The Ten Commandments are like an "owner's manual" for our humanity. Far from being arbitrary or outdated, they are God's way of helping us know how we should live so as to attain true happiness and fulfill the purpose of our existence. What they teach can be known, however imperfectly, by reason. They universally apply to people of all times and places.

Jesus Christ reaffirmed the truth of the Ten Commandments not only by what he said and did, but also by his very identity as the eternal Son of God. By assuming our human nature and becoming one of us, he revealed the Father's love. By doing so, he revealed us to ourselves and showed us who we truly are in the sight of God (see *Gaudium et Spes*, 22). The commandments are thus crucial, not only in our human development, but also in our response to the many ways God calls us to share his life and love.

"I Am the Lord Your God"

Asked by a young man how to attain eternal life, Jesus told him to keep the commandments and then to follow him (Matthew 19:17, 21). We can "rediscover" the truth and permanent validity of the commandments by reflecting on how perfectly Jesus showed their fullest meaning (*Compendium*, 434). In Jesus, the good teacher, the commandments are summed up in loving the Lord with all one's being and loving one's neighbor as oneself (*Compendium*, 435; Matthew 22:37-40).

The Ten Commandments—also called the "Decalogue" or "ten words"—are a summary of the law given to Moses as part of God's covenant with the people of Israel. The first three commandments pertain to love of God, and the remaining seven pertain to love of neighbor. Taken together, the commandments show us the path to freedom from sin so that we can truly love God and neighbor in purity of heart (*Compendium*, 436). Indeed, the commandments are not mere rules. What God asks of his people is that they express their gratitude by doing what is right and good and, in turn, becoming the people he created them to be (437).

Following Jesus, the Church recognizes the fundamental importance of the commandments and teaches us to follow them. The Church also helps us see how they are interrelated and pertain to our duties toward God and our neighbor. Breaking one commandment can seriously weaken our love and dispose us to break others. Although weakened by sin, we are enabled to keep the commandments because of the grace of Christ given to us by the Holy Spirit (*Compendium*, 438–441).

We turn now to the first three commandments, which regard our duty to love God with our entire being. The first is this: "I am the Lord your God. You shall not have other gods before me." Here, we acknowledge the only true and living God through the theological virtues of faith, hope, and charity. Through faith, we believe in God and reject deliberate doubt or unbelief, false teachings (heresy), the total repudiation of the Catholic faith (apostasy), and the willful separation of oneself from the Catholic faith (schism). The virtue of hope "trustingly awaits the blessed vision of God and his help" while avoiding despair or presuming that God will reward us no matter what we do. Charity "loves God above all things" and thus rejects every form of ingratitude and indifference toward God's love. It also rejects laziness in our spiritual life and, above all, hatred of God that is born of pride (*Compendium*, 442).

Worshipping in Spirit and Truth

Both as individuals and as a community of faith, we are to adore and worship God alone. We do so in private prayer and in the celebration of the sacraments, most especially the Mass, and by giving praise to God by how we live. Our human dignity demands that the sincere search for God and one's response to him must be carried out in freedom (*Compendium*, 443–444).

The worship of "false gods" forbidden by the first commandment can take the form of power, money, or pleasure, as well as demon worship. Superstitious beliefs are also opposed to authentic religion. In our day, God is often profaned when religious faith is ridiculed. There is an aggressive atheism that seeks to discredit those who profess belief, and there is also a "practical atheism," when a person decides that not much can be known about God and then proceeds to live as if God does not exist (*Compendium*, 445). The first commandment also forbids idols or false images of God. This does not include things such as images of the Trinity or statutes of the Blessed Virgin Mary and the saints; these are not worshipped but simply serve to remind us of heavenly realities (446).

The second commandment forbids us to take God's name in vain. The name of God is itself holy and worthy of all praise. When someone shows contempt for God's name (blasphemy) or uses God's name as a curse rather than a blessing, God is dishonored. This commandment also forbids us to swear by God's name (*Compendium*, 447–448). In the New Testament, we are told to honor the name of Jesus. In Acts 4:12, for example, we are reminded that there is "no other name" by which the human race can be saved (RSV).

The third commandment tells us to "keep holy the Sabbath." In the story of creation, God "rested" on the seventh day and asked his people to rest. Since Jesus rose from the dead on Sunday, the Sabbath is now celebrated on Sunday. We are to keep Sunday holy by avoiding unnecessary work and by attending Mass (*Compendium*, 450–453). Deliberately missing Sunday Mass violates both the third commandment and the first precept of the Church. Simply put, Christ in the Eucharist must be the center of our lives, and that cannot happen if we are absent from Sunday Mass. Finally, as citizens and believers, we should do all in our power to preserve Sunday as a day of rest and worship.

By following the commandments in the spirit of the Beatitudes, may our lives truly be a living "sacrifice of praise" (Hebrews 13:5).

For Personal Reflection and Group Discussion

1. Do you tend to view the Ten Commandments as rules that restrict your freedom or as the path to freedom from sin? How can you see them as positives rather than negatives?

2. Why are the Ten Commandments for all people in all times and places? How would you explain this idea to someone who might view the commandments as not relevant today?

3. How does the Holy Spirit help us to keep the commandments? How often do you call on the Holy Spirit to help you when you are tempted?

_____

_____

_____

_____

_____

4. Are there any false idols in your life that are keeping you from fully worshipping God? What are some idols in society today that prevent people from following Christ?

_____

_____

_____

_____

_____

5. How do you celebrate the Lord's Day? Is there a way you could make it more special and more a day of rest?

_____

_____

_____

_____

_____

31. The Family in God's Plan

*THE COMMANDMENT TO HONOR ONE'S FATHER AND MOTHER
REFLECTS THE FAMILY'S ROLE IN CHURCH AND SOCIETY*

Compendium: 455–465
Scripture Passage: Deuteronomy 5:16; Sirach 3:2-7, 12-14

The fourth commandment instructs us to "Honor your father and your mother." How many times as youngsters did we confess that we had disobeyed our parents in ways great and small? Yet we can understand this commandment more fully by considering how it encompasses God's entire plan for marriage and family life.

Growing up, I took it for granted that a child's parents consisted of a mother and a father. Today proponents of same-sex marriage and other voices as well tell us that the fourth commandment's reference to one's mother and father is outdated, the product of a bygone culture. However, this perspective hinders us from learning the saving truth of Scripture and from listening to what the voice of reason tells us about marriage and family.

The "Domestic Church"

The *Compendium* reminds us that the family is not merely something invented by human beings. Rather, it is a gift instituted by God and "ordered to the good of the spouses and to the procreation and education of children" (*Compendium*, 456). Indeed, the Church teaches that a couple's capacities to express love and to beget new life are intrinsically linked (Blessed Paul VI, *Humanae Vitae*, 12).

The mutual love of husband and wife, rooted in and strengthened by Christ's love, provides the right environment for begetting and raising children. In the family, children learn life's most basic lessons, including how to respect and love one another, how to tell the truth, and how to grow in virtue. In the family, the faith is taught and imparted, and the family is where children learn to pray. For these reasons, the family is called the "domestic church" (*Compendium*, 456).

In an age when fewer children are growing up in intact families, we must insist that the family, understood as the union of a man and a woman together with their children, is the "original cell" of human society. The faithful, perpetual love of a husband and wife is how children should be brought into the world. Existing prior to all human governments and to its recognition in law, the family plays a unique and irreplaceable role in transmitting virtues and values to young people and in helping them become good and productive citizens (*Compendium*, 457). For that reason, all governments have a duty to respect, protect, and foster authentic marriage and family life. Except for serious reasons such as protecting spouses and children from harm, public authorities should not intervene in family life. At the same time, governments should defend "public morality, the rights of parents, and domestic prosperity" (458).

It would be a mistake for us to think of marriage and family as an easy, idyllic vocation. Mothers and fathers everywhere know better. It takes enormous dedication and energy to form children so that they can accept and fulfill their proper responsibilities. They must be taught by word and example how to relate to God, their families, and society at large.

Likewise, children should learn how to bring harmony to the family circle and to help themselves and the whole family grow in holiness. For example, I know young people whose strong faith persuaded their parents to resume regular attendance at Sunday Mass. Indeed, the duties of children toward their parents extend into adulthood. Adult children should continue to love and revere their parents and provide for them in their advancing years, not just materially, but also emotionally and spiritually, such as by ensuring that they are receiving the sacraments (*Compendium*, 459).

Family Ties

Parents share in God's creative capacity to give life, and from this flows their responsibility to love and respect their children as persons created in God's image and likeness. Accordingly, parents should educate their children and form them in the faith. They do so through prayer, religious instruction within the family, and participation in the Church's life, especially by taking part in the Eucharist each Sunday (*Compendium*, 461).

As the Rite of Infant Baptism explains, "Parents are the first teachers of their children in the ways of faith." They are to provide for their children's material, physical, and spiritual needs, especially their education. It is also important for parents to be open to the vocation that God has in mind for each of their children—be it a lay vocation such as marriage or a religious vocation such as the priesthood—and help guide them toward it, as well as toward an appropriate profession (*Compendium*, 460, 462).

An old saying tells us that "blood is thicker than water." Family bonds run deep, and there is widespread recognition of the need to strengthen them today. Families need to spend time together, share meals, talk with one another, and pray together. At the same time, family ties are not absolute. The first obligation of every family member is to follow and love Jesus Christ. Our love for Christ must exceed even our love for our parents and children (Matthew 10:37).

Within healthy and happy families, an appropriate understanding of authority is more likely to develop, including that of teachers and civil authorities. We are to understand authority as a service to moral truth and the common good, a service that respects human dignity and rights and seeks to create environments conducive to the authentic good of all (*Compendium*, 463–465). In a self-centered culture, this is often hard for people to understand.

Furthermore, parents are to foster in their children habits of good citizenship, including the virtue of patriotism, the right and duty to vote, payment of taxes, and the right to free speech (*Compendium*, 464). And most important, parents are to instill in their children a spirit of service toward others and a readiness to volunteer and assist those in need.

For Personal Reflection and Group Discussion

1. What are the purposes of marriage as instituted by God? What is a healthy family environment meant to foster? Why is it appropriate to call the family the "domestic church"?

2. From your current perspective and experience as an adult, reflect on your relationship with your parents in light of the fourth commandment. What are your obligations toward your parents at this point in your life?

3. What are the duties and responsibilities of parents toward their children? If you are a parent, which of these responsibilities do you find most challenging? Where might you find help, support, or good counsel for better fulfilling your role as a parent?

_____

_____

_____

_____

_____

4. How does your family spend time together? Is this time well used and meaningful, deepening your family's bonds with one another? What might you do to strengthen your family ties?

_____

_____

_____

_____

_____

5. Discuss how contemporary cultural forces are undermining and/ or attempting to redefine marriage and the family. What can you do to safeguard and protect God's plan for marriage and the family?

_____

_____

_____

_____

_____

32. In Defense of Human Life

WE ARE COMMANDED TO PROTECT AND PROMOTE THE GIFT OF HUMAN LIFE AT ALL OF ITS STAGES

Compendium: 466–486
Scripture Passages: Deuteronomy 5:17; Matthew 5:9

The fifth commandment is at the heart of the Church's teaching on the sanctity of human life. It is at the core of the gospel of life, which the Church constantly proclaims in fidelity to her Lord, who came to give us abundant life (John 10:10). The lives that Jesus came to redeem are sacred by their very nature. Each person was created in God's image and likeness and created to enjoy God's friendship.

The starkly negative prohibition "You shall not kill" is meant to protect God's great gift of human life, which should always be treated with respect and love (*Compendium*, 466). As St. John Paul II wrote, "The gift thus becomes a commandment, and the commandment is itself a gift" (*Evangelium Vitae* [The Gospel of Life], 52).

Protecting the Innocent

The Church teaches that there is a legitimate right of self-defense, but it must never be out of rage or use any more force than is necessary. St. John Paul II reminds us of the beautiful witness of those who, while grateful for the gift of life, have laid down their lives for others (*Evangelium Vitae*, 55). Those responsible for the lives of others have not only the right but also the grave duty to defend themselves and those entrusted to their care (*Compendium*, 467).

Moreover, public authorities may legitimately punish those who break the law so as to protect public safety and correct offenders (*Compendium*, 468). Such punishment must be proportionate to the crime. Today, because there are means other than capital punishment to protect society from dangerous criminals, both the Church and many segments of society have reached the conclusion that as a practical matter, capital punishment should no longer be administered (469).

The fifth commandment unequivocally forbids the taking of innocent human life, from conception to natural death. The Church is clear that no one is permitted to ask for, or even consent to, the killing of an innocent human being—whether at the beginning, middle, or end of life. "Nor can any authority legitimately recommend or permit such an action" (Congregation for the Doctrine of the Faith, *Declaration on Euthanasia*, 2; *Compendium*, 470).

Pro-life initiatives are inspired by the conviction that the Creator, not the state, endows each person with the inalienable right to life. Laws that permit abortion are inherently unjust and weaken "the very foundations of a State based on law" (*Compendium*, 472).

As health care becomes more and more complex, questions arise about appropriate levels of care. Experimental treatments and organ transplants are morally acceptable as long as the risks are not disproportionate and the patient or donor, when fully informed, gives consent (*Compendium*, 475). Organ donation after death is "a noble act," but before organs are removed, the death of the donor must be verified (476).

For the chronically ill and those near death, ordinary medical care should not be interrupted. It is legitimate to administer drugs to manage pain but not to hasten death. There is no moral obligation to employ drugs and medical procedures without reasonable expectation that they will benefit the patient (*Compendium*, 471). "Right to die" legislation that seeks to legalize euthanasia must be strongly resisted.

The dying should always be given loving care and supported by prayer and the sacraments so that they might be prepared to meet God (*Compendium*, 477). Believing in the resurrection of the body, we are to treat the bodies of the deceased with love and respect.

Cremation is permitted as long as it is not a way of denying belief in the resurrection of the body (479).

Seeking Peace

The fifth commandment also bids us to be peacemakers. This requires that each of us renounce hatred and seek to build bonds of understanding and friendship in a fractured world (*Compendium*, 480). More than the absence of war, peace calls for a society that is both just and charitable (482).

Yet we also face the question of when it is legitimate to use military force. The conditions for a just war remain: (1) the suffering inflicted by the aggressor must be lasting, grave, and certain; (2) all other peaceful means must be shown to be ineffective; (3) there are well-founded prospects of success; and (4) the use of arms, especially weapons of mass destruction, must not produce evils greater than the evil to be eliminated (*Compendium*, 483). Governments have an obligation to adhere strictly to these standards, even as they have the right to ask citizens to defend their homeland.

Governments also have the duty to respect conscientious objectors; those who do not engage in national defense in time of war should perform some other community service (*Compendium*, 484). We should be grateful to those who bravely defend their country and remember those who have paid the ultimate price to defend human freedom and dignity.

In time of war, every effort must be made to treat innocent civilians, wounded soldiers, and prisoners of war humanely. The provisions of international law must be respected. All acts of mass destruction and the extermination of minorities or religious groups are utterly grievous evils. Orders to engage in such acts should not be obeyed (*Compendium*, 485).

In view of the crimes and atrocities that occur in wartime, we must do everything possible to avoid war. Our commitment to charity, fraternity, and unity should prompt us to root out "all forms of economic and social injustice; ethnic and religious discrimination; envy, mistrust, pride and the spirit of revenge" (*Compendium*, 486). In all these ways, we are to live the gospel of life and propose it convincingly to the world.

For Personal Reflection and Group Discussion

1. Do you view life as sacred and as a gift from God? In what ways might you be tempted to think that some lives are of greater value than others? In what ways does society exhibit this tendency?

_____

_____

_____

_____

_____

2. Why, in most cases, does the Church believe that capital punishment should no longer be administered? Is this a difficult teaching for you to accept? Why or why not?

_____

_____

_____

_____

_____

3. How might you support pro-life initiatives, even if you don't have the time to be actively involved? How can you witness to the gospel of life to others?

_____

_____

_____

_____

_____

4. How might Catholics promote the gospel of life and contribute to the building up of earthly peace and a just and charitable society, even in small ways?

_____

_____

_____

_____

_____

5. What conditions must be present for the use of military force to be justifiable and morally permitted? What more do you think the government should be doing to avoid war and promote justice? What can you do?

_____

_____

_____

_____

_____

33. God's Plan for Life and Love

THE VIRTUE OF CHASTITY IS NECESSARY TO PROTECT AND PRACTICE THE TRUTH ABOUT MARRIAGE, SEXUALITY, AND HUMAN LIFE

Compendium: 487–502; 527–530
Scripture Passages: Deuteronomy 5:18; Matthew 5:27-28

The very notion of chastity is unpopular in contemporary culture. It is often equated with sexual repression and is decidedly out of step with how sexuality is portrayed by the entertainment industry. The *Compendium*, however, introduces to us a very different way of looking at chastity. It is a gift from God and a virtue by which we integrate our sexual powers and attain the self-mastery necessary to give ourselves in love and service to others (488–489). It is an essential part of building a culture of life.

Chastity is not reserved for only a few; all of the baptized are called to model their lives on Christ by being formed in this virtue, which is to be practiced in all states of life or vocations within the Church. This formation takes place through the sacraments, prayer, mortification (such as fasting), and exercising the moral virtues, especially the virtue of temperance, by which our passions are steadily controlled by reason (*Compendium*, 490).

A Divine Purpose

Some, such as religious and priests, profess virginity or consecrated celibacy so as to serve God and the Church with an undivided heart. While the unmarried are also called to refrain from sexual activity reserved for marriage, married couples are called to conjugal chastity, or purity within marriage. At a minimum, this enjoins them to refrain from all sexual activity outside of marriage (*Compendium*, 491). These are not merely man-made rules. Rather, they help us model our lives after Christ and the Beatitudes: "Blessed are the pure in heart, for they shall see God" (Matthew 5:8, RSV).

Chastity respects the intertwined, God-given purposes of human sexuality, which are to express the exclusive love of husband and wife in a manner that is open to the procreation of new human life (*Compendium*, 496). As Blessed Paul VI warned in his 1968 encyclical *Humanae Vitae*, separating sexuality's power to express married love and to beget new life has opened the door to abortion and many other assaults on the family, on the truth of sexuality, and on the dignity of human life.

The sixth commandment, "You shall not commit adultery," forbids all expressions of the vice known as lust, including adultery, masturbation, fornication, pornography, prostitution, rape, and homosexual acts. When such acts are committed against a minor by an adult, their gravity is intensified (*Compendium*, 492). Sexual abuse on the part of those who represent the Church is particularly reprehensible, and in recent years, the Church has taken appropriate steps to protect children and young people.

The Church's teaching on chastity has often been held up to ridicule and distortion. This was true in the decades following the so-called sexual revolution of the late 1960s and remains true today. In addition, there has been a trend in courts and legislatures to legalize as a human "right" sexual acts that are, in fact, destructive. In such cases, civil authorities have abdicated their responsibility to create a society that fully respects human dignity and the institution of marriage while protecting the most vulnerable (*Compendium*, 494). Unfortunately, young people are sometimes permitted and encouraged, even by their parents and public-school authorities, to engage in sexual activity, while formation in chastity is dismissed as "unworkable."

Mutual Self-Gift

Despite the fact that chastity is often distorted in our culture, it is at the heart of the vocation of marriage. Our human sexuality is not merely a means to pleasure but is instead ordered toward the benefits of married love: unity, fidelity, indissolubility, and openness to new life (*Compendium*, 495). Accordingly, God has invested two inseparable meanings to the conjugal act: the unitive meaning—the mutual self-giving of the husband and wife; and the procreative meaning—openness to the transmission of new life (496). Actions such as sterilization and contraception, which break the intrinsic connection between these two meanings, are immoral and contrary to God's plan for human life (498).

Of course, there can be morally sound reasons for a husband and wife to regulate the timing and number of births in their family. These decisions must not be made for selfish reasons or as the result of external pressures, and must be carried out by morally licit methods, which involve continence during periods when the wife is fertile (*Compendium*, 497). Couples who struggle with the Church's teaching in this regard should be provided generous pastoral help and encouragement.

The efforts of infertile couples to have children must also respect the link between the unitive and procreative meanings of the conjugal act. Procedures such as artificial insemination and artificial fertilization, or methods that involve using a third party to carry a child to term, are morally illicit. Children are a gift from God; no couple has a "right" to a child, and no couple should regard a child as an intolerable burden (*Compendium*, 499–500). By contrast, from the moment of conception, children do indeed have a God-given "right to life." When a husband and wife generously seek to have children but find, after exploring all legitimate options, that they cannot do so, they should consider the possibility of adoption and avenues of service to others (501).

Offenses against the dignity of marriage also include acts such as adultery, divorce, polygamy, incest, cohabitation, sexual acts before or outside of marriage, and so-called same-sex marriage (*Compendium*, 502).

We should ask for the grace to open our minds and hearts to the truth and beauty of the Church's challenging and life-giving teaching on human sexuality. We are called to embrace this teaching and to lead others to live the virtue of chastity in generosity and joy.

For Personal Reflection and Group Discussion

1. Discuss together or reflect on the meaning of chastity and the integrity of the human person. Why is chastity considered a gift from God and a virtue?

_____

_____

_____

_____

_____

2. Why are all persons called to live chastely, in keeping with their vocation and particular state of life? How can this idea be best communicated to young people?

_____

_____

_____

_____

_____

3. Why do you think the attitude that children are a "right" prevails in our society? How does viewing a child as a gift from God change how we think about the use of certain artificial means to achieve conception?

_____

_____

_____

_____

_____

4. Why does the Church teach that some means of regulating birth or achieving conception are immoral and contrary to God's plan for human life? What resources could you explore to achieve a deeper understanding of this teaching?

_____

_____

_____

_____

_____

5. Contemporary culture holds many distorted views about human sexuality and widely endorses practices that are offenses against the sixth commandment. Discuss what you or your parish might do to support the Church's teachings on human sexuality and to foster and safeguard the dignity of marriage.

_____

_____

_____

_____

_____

34. Stewardship of This World's Goods

Our Work and Civic Responsibilities Are Rooted in Human Dignity and the Common Good

Compendium: 503–520; 531–533
Scripture Passages: Deuteronomy 5:19, 21; Matthew 6:21

The moral ground covered by the seventh commandment—"You shall not steal"—includes the right to private property, respect for creation, the Church's social doctrine, the dignity of human work, justice and solidarity among nations, participation in political life, and love for the poor (*Compendium*, 503). Closely related is the tenth commandment, which enjoins us from coveting the possessions and attainments of others (531–533). Taken together, these two commandments instruct us to be just and generous stewards of God's blessings. They also help us to see what it means to love our neighbor and to work with others in creating a just and well-ordered society.

Private Property

We sense a right to own what we have justly acquired, especially those possessions for which we have worked and paid. But we also sense that the right to private property is not boundless (*Compendium*, 504). Recall the rich man in Luke's Gospel who had no regard for Lazarus, a poor man who lacked basic necessities (16:19-31). In asserting the right to private ownership, the Church also asks us to be temperate in using the world's goods. Indeed, the right to own private property is an expression of human dignity. The purpose of this right is to meet the basic necessities of life, including one's own needs; the needs of those for whom one is responsible, such as family members; and the needs of others (505).

Respecting what belongs to others brings into play several virtues, notably justice and charity, together with temperance and solidarity. Our dealings with others should be marked by a readiness to keep our word and to honor the terms of legitimate contracts we have entered into. Abiding by the seventh commandment requires that we make amends for injustices we have committed and return what we have stolen. It also demands that we have genuine concern for the needs of others and a desire to use this world's goods in a careful, prudent way, out of respect for creation and concern for others (*Compendium*, 506).

The *Compendium* points out that there are many ways we can take what does not belong to us, such as paying unjust wages, undertaking risky or dishonest investments that put others at a disadvantage, participating in tax evasion or fraudulent business practices, performing shoddy labor, damaging private or public property, or creating waste (508). Only a moment's reflection tells us that such dishonest practices harm not only individuals, but also the common good of society. We only have to think of the role that greed and fear played in bringing about the global recession.

Pope Francis often reminds us that the Church speaks to social and economic problems to defend human dignity and to guide citizens and their leaders in constructing a just society. Accordingly, the Church teaches that economic and financial systems must be conducted ethically and be at the service of the human person, not the other way around (*Compendium*, 511). Both the unbridled quest for profit in the marketplace and the untrammeled exercise of power by totalitarian governments offend human dignity (512).

Dignity and Justice

It is the duty of the state to oversee social and economic systems in such a way that they respect the right and duty of human persons to secure and honest employment, open to all without unjust discrimination. As such, the state should foster economic growth and provide conditions under which workers are justly compensated (*Compendium*, 514–515). We are called to be diligent and competent in our daily work, by which we are cooperating with God, the Creator of all things. Labor is a very important way of providing for our families and contributing to the common good of society. It is also a path toward holiness (513).

Respect for human work requires the cooperation of both management and labor. In legitimately seeking business opportunities and profits, managers must also compensate workers fairly and provide for decent working conditions. For their part, workers are to be conscientious and diligent in carrying out their tasks. To the extent possible, labor disputes should be resolved by good-faith negotiations on the part of management and those who represent workers. When such negotiations break down, a nonviolent strike that aims at just compensation and working conditions cannot be ruled out; such action, however, must not endanger the common good, including the health and safety of others (*Compendium*, 516–517).

These days no economy or financial system stands alone—we are linked in a global economy. As a result, every nation, particularly those that are wealthy and powerful, is obliged to work for economic justice and a decent standard of living throughout the world (*Compendium*, 518). For this to come about, however, citizens must actively engage in civic affairs as witnesses to authentic gospel values (519).

To be stewards of God's gifts after the mind and heart of Christ, we must embrace the Beatitudes. This means imitating Christ's own spirit of detachment from this world's goods, together with charity for the poor and needy (*Compendium*, 520, 532). Indeed, the great desire of our lives must be not for material gain but rather to live in God's presence (533). Virtues such as charity, unity, and fraternity help us to be those good and loving stewards of God's gifts so that at the end of our lives, we may hear the Master say to us, "Well done, my good and faithful servant" (Matthew 25:23).

For Personal Reflection and Group Discussion

1. Have you ever thought that taking what does not belong to us encompasses those things listed in this chapter and in the *Compendium* (508)? Why are they important to consider as we examine our own hearts?

_____

_____

_____

_____

_____

2. Why is the right to private property limited? Why is it an expression of human dignity?

_____

_____

_____

_____

_____

3. How well are you exercising stewardship over your personal goods and property? Do you use your possessions wisely and for the good of others? In what areas might you be more generous?

_____

_____

_____

_____

_____

4. Examine your attitudes and practices toward creation—animals, plants, nature, and the resources of the earth. What might you do to better preserve the earth's resources for future generations?

_____

_____

_____

_____

_____

5. How might you better practice detachment from the world's goods, in imitation of Jesus? What practical steps could you take to grow in this area?

_____

_____

_____

_____

_____

35. Living in Truth

CHRISTIANS HAVE A RESPONSIBILITY TO PRACTICE HONESTY AND INTEGRITY IN ALL THAT THEY DO

Compendium: 521–526
Scripture Passages: Deuteronomy 5:20; Matthew 5:33-37

Experience teaches us that "honesty is the best policy." A moment's reflection reminds us of the importance of honesty and integrity in our personal lives, our work, and our relationships. When our word is our bond, we build trust, engender cooperation, and serve the common good.

Truthfulness, of course, is not just a matter of words; it is a way of life. St. Paul speaks of "living the truth in love" (Ephesians 4:15), and Pope Benedict XVI aptly named his encyclical on the Church's social teaching *Caritas in Veritate* (Charity in Truth). We must seek to live the truth in charity and charity in truth.

By contrast, experience teaches how destructive deception can be. How many marriages, careers, businesses, and institutions have been tarnished or ruined by a lack of honesty? Deception complicates life and undermines a person's good work. Yet in a highly competitive and self-centered culture that is often marked by greed and fear, it is easy for people to fall into the habit of telling lies.

The *Compendium* helps us see that each person has a duty to sincerely seek the truth and to live according to it.

Hide Nothing from God

We know that Jesus is "the way and the truth and the life" (John 14:6). As followers of Christ, therefore, we must guard against duplicity, deception, and hypocrisy (*Compendium*, 521).

Among other things, this means that we must not compartmentalize our lives, hiding aspects of our lives from the truth of God's word. For example, a man may appear to be a loving spouse and father at home but still be a scoundrel at work. Eventually, his bad behavior at work will impinge on his family. Thus, a Christian "must bear witness to the truth of the Gospel in every field of his activity, both public and private, and also if necessary, with the sacrifice of his very life" (*Compendium*, 522).

Each of us must ask for the light of Christ's grace to shine in the darkened corners of our souls so that we hide nothing from God or ourselves. In doing so, we bear witness to Christ's truth and love to others with a clear conscience. Fundamental to this witness is observing the eighth commandment—"You shall not bear false witness against your neighbor."

This commandment forbids all forms of deception and dishonesty, including false witness, perjury, and lying. False witness means providing dishonest testimony either for or against another person; perjury refers to lying under oath, such as in a court of law; and lying is defined as failing to tell the truth, speaking an outright falsehood, or distorting the truth in the ordinary circumstances of daily life (*Compendium*, 523).

Of course, some lies are more serious than others. Perjury on the part of a witness that sends an innocent defendant to prison for the rest of his life is more serious than lying about one's age. "Gilding the lily" when trying to help a colleague land a job is less serious than speaking falsehoods that lead to a co-worker being fired. The gravity of false witness, perjury, or any lie "is measured by the truth it deforms, the circumstances, the intentions of the one who lies, and the harm suffered by its victims" (*Compendium*, 523).

Justice and Charity

The eighth commandment also forbids rash judgment, slander, defamation, and calumny. Jesus has shown us a love that is patient and merciful, yet it is easy for us to judge others and engage in gossip that tears down their reputation. Whether this gossip is true, false, or only partially true, what these immoral forms of speech have in common is their maliciousness—the use of one's tongue as a weapon. This has no place in our lives as followers of Christ.

Then there is flattery, adulation, and complaisance. Flattery and adulation involve paying undue compliments or heaping false praise upon others. Both are dishonest ways of speaking aimed at reaping some advantage that we would otherwise not acquire. Complaisance has to do with being overly agreeable to another's wishes or actions, even when we know them to be morally flawed (*Compendium*, 523).

Obeying the eighth commandment, of course, does not mean telling everyone everything we know. Rather, it "requires respect for the truth accompanied by the discretion of charity" (*Compendium*, 524). Those who work in the media have a responsibility to present information that is "true and—within the limits of justice and charity—also complete" (525). Yet in today's twenty-four-hour news cycle and the world of social networking, information is often shared without any regard for legitimate privacy rights, human dignity, or the common good. Things such as doctor-patient confidentiality should be observed, and information given under the seal of secrecy should be respected (524).

Finally, works of art should also lead us to the truth. St. John Paul II captured the relationship between truth and beauty in the title of his 1993 encyclical on morality, *Veritatis Splendor*. That which is true is beautiful, and that which is truly beautiful is true. Thus, artistic works, including painting and music, should evoke something of the truth and beauty of God. In this connection, we can readily see the importance of religious art, which is aimed at glorifying God, whose beauty, truth, and love were "made visible in Christ" (*Compendium*, 526).

The ninth commandment, "You shall not covet your neighbor's wife," forbids "cultivating thoughts and desires connected to actions forbidden by the sixth commandment" (*Compendium*, 528), which was discussed in chapter 33. The tenth commandment,

"You shall not covet your neighbor's possessions," which was discussed in chapter 34, forbids "greed, unbridled covetousness for the goods of others, and envy" (531). Instead, it calls us to "detachment from riches—in the spirit of evangelical poverty—and self-abandonment to divine providence" (532).

For Personal Reflection and Group Discussion

1. What is your duty toward truth? How well are you seeking to live the truth in love? Do you think others would say that your life bears witness to truth? To the gospel and to your faith? Why or why not?

2. Recall an instance when you acted with integrity and honesty, and consider how this made a positive difference to you and to others. Also recall an instance when acting with honesty or keeping your word cost you in some way (for example, you suffered ridicule, rejection by others, or financial hardship). What good came out of your upright behavior?

3. Have you ever been the victim of deception, duplicity, or dishonesty or had your good name or reputation slandered? How did you respond?

_____

_____

_____

_____

_____

4. We all struggle with using our speech to build up rather than tear down. How often do you slip into gossip or negative comments about someone? How often do you blurt out something that would have been better left unsaid? Ask the Lord for forgiveness as well as for his grace and help to better guard your tongue.

_____

_____

_____

_____

_____

5. Reflect on the relationship that exists between truth, beauty, and sacred art. Share with the group a favorite work of art or a piece of music that communicates something of the beauty and truth of God to you. What response to God does this evoke from you? Gratitude? Worship? Awe?

_____

_____

_____

_____

_____

36. Prayer: A Gift from God

Scripture Teaches Us the Meaning of Prayer and Presents Us with Models of Discipleship

Compendium: 534–547
Scripture Passage: John 17:1-26

The fourth and final section of the *Compendium* discusses the topic of prayer in the Christian life. Prayer is defined as "the raising of one's mind and heart to God, or the petition of good things from him in accord with his will" (534). In prayer we turn our whole attention to God, offer him praise, and, seeking only his will, ask for what we need. We are obliged to pray, but prayer is also God's gift to us. It is how we grow in our friendship with Christ who, in the power of the Holy Spirit, leads us to the Father of mercies. Prayer is also how we support one another in the challenges of life; we should often seek the prayers of others, and we should generously remember the needs of others in our prayers.

In a sense, prayer is something natural. Each human being is created in God's image, and in spite of original sin, every person retains a desire for God. Yet it is God who seeks our friendship and draws us to himself.

Prayer in the Bible

The Old Testament presents Abraham—our father in faith—as a model of prayer because he walked in God's presence, listened to him, and obeyed his will. Like Abraham, Moses frequently interceded before God on behalf of the chosen people. Moses' strength as a leader, however, came from his uniquely intimate relationship with God. God called Moses from the burning bush and spoke to him in a remarkably direct manner, especially during the encounter on Mount Sinai (Exodus 3:1-15; 19:1-25). Because of his constant, intimate communication with God, Moses is seen as a model of contemplative prayer (*Compendium*, 537).

Those who shepherded the people of Israel helped them see that God dwelt in their midst. Foremost among these leaders is David, the shepherd and king "after [God's] own heart" (Acts 13:22). Sacred tradition holds that David's faith was the inspiration for the psalms, the greatest prayers in the Old Testament. Inspired by the Holy Spirit, the psalms are the word of God given to us as our own prayer. They sing of God's goodness in creating the world and his promise of redemption. They were prayed by Jesus and are at the heart of the Church's prayer (*Compendium*, 540).

The Old Testament also shows us how the prophets prayed. Like Moses, they entered deeply into prayer before the living God. Overshadowed by the spirit of the Lord, they received the word of the Lord so that they could speak to the people on God's behalf.

Above all, it was in Jesus Christ that God our Father taught us what prayer is and how to pray. Both Son of God and Son of Mary, Jesus lived in obedience with Mary and Joseph in their home in Nazareth. There, in his human nature, he learned from his mother how to pray. But as the eternal Son of God, his prayer had an even deeper source (*Compendium*, 541; John 1:14).

In the New Testament, we frequently find Jesus absorbed in prayer. He fasted and prayed for forty days and nights before he began his public ministry and prayed before choosing his apostles (Matthew 4:2; Luke 6:12). He often withdrew from the crowds to pray and taught his disciples the importance of doing so (Mark 6:31). Jesus, who taught us to pray constantly, made his whole life a prayer to his Father in heaven (1 Thessalonians 5:17; *Compendium*, 542).

"Lord, Teach Us to Pray"

Jesus' prayer reached its pinnacle in his passion and death. During the agony in the garden, Jesus suffered intensely as he took upon himself the sins of the world and the anguish of a suffering humanity. In obedience to the Father's will, he laid down his life to save us. There he experienced for us the full weight of our sinful alienation from his Father and from one another. In this moment of supreme suffering on the cross, Jesus interceded for us, and the Father heard his prayer and answered it "beyond all hope by raising his Son from the dead" (*Compendium*, 543).

So that we could pray as he did, in harmony with the Father's will, Jesus gave us the Our Father as the perfect pattern of prayer. At the same time, he showed us the interior attitudes we should have when we pray, most especially purity of heart, openness to God's will, love even for one's enemies, and an intrepid faith and vigilance against temptation (*Compendium*, 544). The interior dispositions needed for prayer are beautifully summarized in the Beatitudes.

This leads us back to the truth that prayer is God's gift to us. Our prayer is pleasing to the Father when, in the power of the Holy Spirit, it is united to the prayer of Jesus. In this way, prayer deepens our communion with the Holy Trinity.

Finally, just as Mary taught Jesus to pray, so she also helps us pray. Before she conceived the Son of God in her womb, she prayed in complete openness to the living word of God. Thus, she was prepared to share fully in the mission of Christ. Each day the Church repeats Mary's beautiful prayer of thanksgiving, the Magnificat (Luke 1:46-55). Mary prayed with the apostles at Pentecost and was present at the first Eucharistic celebrations (Acts 2:42). Her prayers for us and for all our needs are loving and powerful (*Compendium*, 546–547). Of particular importance and beauty is the Rosary, in which through Mary's eyes we contemplate the great events, the mysteries of life of Christ, while beseeching her intercession. She always leads us to Jesus. May Mary intercede for us so that we may grow in the ways of prayer.

For Personal Reflection and Group Discussion

1. Why is it right and appropriate to call prayer a gift of God? What does this express to you about God's desire for us to be united to him?

   _____

   _____

   _____

   _____

   _____

2. Define prayer in your own words. How would you describe your own prayer?

   _____

   _____

   _____

   _____

   _____

3. What can we learn about how to pray from the prayer of Abraham and Moses as described in the Old Testament? What place do the psalms have in your prayer life?

   _____

   _____

   _____

   _____

   _____

4. Discuss several examples of how Jesus prayed as recounted in the Gospels. Which scene of Jesus at prayer is especially meaningful to you right now? Why? In what ways is your own prayer modeled after that of Jesus?

_____

_____

_____

_____

_____

5. What place do you give to prayer in your daily life and schedule? How might you be more open and attentive to the Lord in prayer?

_____

_____

_____

_____

_____

37. The Essentials of Prayer

GUIDED BY THE HOLY SPIRIT AND THE CHURCH, WE LEARN TO PRAISE, THANK, AND PRESENT OUR NEEDS TO GOD

Compendium: 548–565
Scripture Passage: Romans 8:26-27; Psalm 145

The memory that I cherish most of St. John Paul II was the privilege of seeing him absorbed in prayer in his private chapel prior to Mass. His prayer was deeply personal yet was completely tied to the Church's life of prayer, rooted in the living word of God and in the celebration of the Eucharist. St. John Paul II gave us a wonderful example of how the Holy Spirit forms the whole Church in prayer and in the ever-deeper contemplation of the mystery of Christ (*Compendium*, 548–549).

Guided by the Holy Spirit, the Church teaches and practices the essential forms of prayer, which are most perfectly found in the Eucharist: blessing and adoration; petition and intercession; thanksgiving and praise (*Compendium*, 550).

Prayer and Tradition

In the prayer of blessing, it is God who first blesses us and enables us to "bless" him (*Compendium*, 551). Because God fills us with his gifts, we can live the Beatitudes and say with the psalmist: "Bless the LORD, my soul; / all my being, bless his holy name!" (Psalm 103:1). The prayer of adoration is a humble acknowledgment that we are creatures of God who owe our very existence and salvation to his goodness and generosity (552).

In the prayer of petition, we present our spiritual and material needs. Jesus taught us first to ask for the coming of his kingdom, which is realized in us when, through grace, we keep the commandments in the spirit of the Beatitudes. Seeking to live the heart of the gospel, we ask God to forgive our sins and we pray—not merely for the things we *want*, but for those things we truly *need* to grow in the likeness of Christ (*Compendium*, 553).

One of the most beautiful ways we can follow Christ is to pray, or intercede, for one another, just as the risen and exalted Lord pleads for us at the right hand of the Father (Romans 8:34). Our prayer of intercession should include not only our family and friends, but also our enemies, for Jesus taught, "Love your enemies, and pray for those who persecute you" (Matthew 5:44; *Compendium*, 554).

At the heart of all Christian prayer is thanksgiving. On our own, we cannot thank God as we should, but in the Eucharist we join in Christ's prayer of thanksgiving to God the Father (*Compendium*, 555). Closely tied to thanksgiving is praise. Loving God above all things, we joyfully acknowledge God's greatness and glory (556). A spirit of praise and thanksgiving should permeate our whole lives.

As Christians, we never pray alone but rather always as part of the Church's tradition and in union with our fellow believers and disciples. In fact, it is through this tradition and returning to the sources of Christian prayer that the Holy Spirit teaches us to pray (*Compendium*, 557). Our prayer is rooted in Scripture, the word of God that leads us to "the supreme good of knowing Christ" (Philippians 3:8), and in the Church's liturgy, which communicates through sacramental signs the saving words and deeds of Christ.

Learning to Pray

In Baptism, the Holy Spirit pours forth into our hearts the theological virtues of faith, hope, and love. In this way the Spirit teaches us to pray and enables us to believe in God, instilling in us a desire for the joy of God's kingdom and a love for God above all things (CCC, 1814; 1817; 1822). When we truly know, love, and practice our faith, everyday situations become occasions for prayer. This is what St. Paul means when he tells us to "pray without ceasing" (1 Thessalonians 5:17; *Compendium*, 558).

There are, of course, many ways to pray. For example, we might be familiar with popular devotions that are tied to a particular country or culture. Pope Francis reminds us of the important role that popular devotions play in spreading the gospel and in forming disciples capable of evangelizing (*Evangelii Gaudium*, 122–126). We also look to the Church to guide our prayer so as to ensure that it is centered on the Person of Christ (*Compendium*, 559).

In fact, Jesus is "the way" of prayer. During his life on earth, he prayed constantly, and he continues to plead for us from his place in heaven. It is through the humanity of God's divine Son that the Holy Spirit teaches us to pray, and we always make our prayer "through our Lord Jesus Christ" (*Compendium*, 560). What is more, it is the Spirit who is "the artisan" and "interior Master" of all prayer. The Spirit teaches us to "pray as we ought" by leading us to Christ and pouring forth divine life into our souls (561; Romans 8:26).

At the same time, our prayer is always united with that of Mary. All generations call her blessed and echo her prayer of praise and thanksgiving, the Magnificat (Luke 1:46-55). Mary leads us to Jesus with maternal love and prays for us with special tenderness. We invoke her intercession through the Hail Mary, the Rosary, and many other beautiful prayers (*Compendium*, 562–563). We also look to the saints, many of whom were great masters of the spiritual life, to teach us how to pray. In interceding for us in heaven, the saints shine with the glory of Christ (564).

Finally, the home should be a school of prayer, just as Jesus learned to pray in his home in Nazareth. Parents are the first teachers of their children in the ways of faith (*Compendium*, 565).

For Personal Reflection and Group Discussion

1. Is thanksgiving at the heart of your prayer? How can you grow more in gratitude for all that the Lord has done for you? How can spending time in prayer and with Scripture help in this regard?

_____

_____

_____

_____

_____

2. Do you praise God in your prayer? Why is praise important? Could you grow in this area by using praise music in your prayer or by praying psalms of praise?

_____

_____

_____

_____

_____

3. How much of your prayer is taken up in interceding for others? Do you let others know you are praying for them? Do you pray for your "enemies" or those with whom you have difficult relationships?

_____

_____

_____

_____

_____

4. How do you rely on the Holy Spirit to lead you in prayer? Share
   with others practical ways to do this.

   _____

   _____

   _____

   _____

   _____

5. How is your own prayer united with that of Mary? In what ways
   does Mary serve as a model for prayer?

   _____

   _____

   _____

   _____

   _____

38. How to Pray Better

*The Practice of Prayer Disposes Us to Receive the
Gift of Faith and Grow in Friendship with God*

Compendium: 566–577
Scripture Passage: Psalm 27

Catholics who know and love their faith will often say that they have difficulty making time to pray or that they find themselves distracted when they do try to pray. To strengthen our life of prayer, the *Compendium* offers practical guidance from the great masters of the spiritual life and from the Lord himself.

Let's begin with *where* to pray. The celebration of Mass and the sacraments, as well as Eucharistic adoration, should normally take place in a church or chapel that has been properly arranged and suitably adorned. Private prayer, on the other hand, can take place anywhere. For instance, a person might pray the Rosary in a car or on a train. However, to foster a habit of daily prayer, it is good to set aside a place at home, which might be as simple as a favorite chair or a small room that affords a bit of privacy. Not to be forgotten, of course, is the importance of going to churches and shrines in order to visit the Blessed Sacrament (*Compendium*, 566).

Three Forms of Prayer

Jesus tells us to pray "without becoming weary" (Luke 18:1), and St. Paul advises us to "pray without ceasing" (1 Thessalonians 5:17). Does this mean that we should cease our daily activity and simply pray? Whereas contemplative religious spend much of their day absorbed in prayer, most of us are called to punctuate our day with prayer so that everything we say or do is animated by a prayerful spirit (*Compendium*, 576). That is why we should pray in the morning and evening, before and after meals, and when we are facing some difficulty or temptation. The daily prayerful reading of Scripture is a treasured and fruitful way to pray, as is the Rosary. Laypeople also profit greatly from praying the Liturgy of the Hours, which clergy and religious are required to pray (567).

In general, there are three forms of prayer: vocal prayer, meditation, and contemplative prayer. Each of these requires us to focus on God and his loving kindness, cultivating a heart that is free from distraction (*Compendium*, 568).

Vocal prayer involves praying with particular words, either mentally or out loud. We use our powers of speech to give voice to prayer, wishing to give thanks and praise to God and to ask for the graces necessary to grow in holiness. The Our Father, which Jesus taught us to pray, is the perfect form of vocal prayer and will be the focus of our next chapter (*Compendium*, 569).

Meditation comes from the Latin word *meditatio*, which means "thinking over." A reflective form of prayer, it often begins with reading the word of God and allowing it to resonate in our minds and hearts. Meditation engages our powers of thought and imagination as well as our emotions and desires. It marshals our interior powers to focus on the mysteries of our faith and on God's will for our lives. The practice of daily mediation is a very important way to grow in holiness (*Compendium*, 570).

Finally, contemplative prayer is a prayer beyond words, in which we simply gaze upon the Lord in silence and love. It might be likened to the loving silence of a happily married husband and wife who no longer need a lot of words to convey their oneness of mind and heart. Contemplative prayer is a gift of the Holy Spirit that leads us to trustfully surrender ourselves to the Lord and his will for us. The practice of contemplative prayer, as St. Teresa of Avila teaches us, is an indication of our growing friendship with Christ (*Compendium*, 571).

Praying with Vigilance

If prayer is beautiful and life-giving, why is it often difficult? Why must we battle with distractions and temptations to cut our prayer short or to not pray at all? Of course, Satan does not want us to pray and would prefer that we focus on ourselves rather than on "what is above" (Colossians 3:2). Because of our human weakness, we are only too willing to submit to these temptations. Prayer is a grace that engages our willpower, since we have to pray even when we don't feel like doing so (*Compendium*, 572).

Likewise, we sometimes might be tempted to think that God isn't listening or that he is rejecting our pleas. At other times, we find ourselves so distracted that we want to give up praying altogether. Or we may wonder why our prayer is "dry," that is, lacking in consolation. But prayer requires both vigilance and perseverance. When we pray almost in spite of ourselves, with humility and trust, we grow in faith and friendship with Christ. We are drawn ever more deeply into his life and love.

Prayer also requires a repentant and trusting heart. We can become lazy about praying or experience difficulty with prayer because we are not willing to repent of our sins (*Compendium*, 573–574). With the psalmist we must often say, "A clean heart create for me, God; / renew within me a steadfast spirit" (Psalm 51:12). The more steadfastly we pray in faith, hope, and love, the more the Holy Spirit will transform our hearts and make evident the fruits of the Spirit in our lives (575).

Jesus prayed throughout his life and especially at the divinely appointed time of his passion and death. We should pray so as to enter into this prayer of Jesus, which he continuously offers for us at the right hand of the Father (*Compendium*, 577).

For Personal Reflection and Group Discussion

1. Share about places you find to be conducive to prayer. Have you set aside a suitable place in your home where you are able to pray?

   _____

   _____

   _____

   _____

   _____

2. How important or meaningful to you is vocal prayer—alone or in groups? Is your vocal prayer "from the heart" or has it become rote or routine?

   _____

   _____

   _____

   _____

   _____

3. How has meditative prayer deepened your relationship with the Lord? Why is contemplative prayer called a "gaze of faith" and "a gaze of love"?

   _____

   _____

   _____

   _____

   _____

4. What do you find to be most difficult about praying? Finding time in your schedule? Distractions? Dryness? Feeling that God is absent? Discuss together ways to address and/or overcome these difficulties.

_____

_____

_____

_____

_____

5. What impact has the practice of daily prayer had on you? In what ways has prayer transformed you and/or borne fruit in your life?

_____

_____

_____

_____

39. The Lord's Prayer

*WITH THE OUR FATHER, JESUS BOTH TAUGHT US HOW
TO PRAY AND GAVE US A SUMMARY OF THE GOSPEL*

Compendium: 578–598
Scripture Passage: Matthew 6:9-13; Luke 11:1-4

Observing Jesus at prayer, his disciples asked him for instruction on how to pray (Luke 11:1). In response, Jesus taught them a prayer so familiar to us that we often say the words without reflecting on their meaning. Fittingly, the *Compendium* concludes with a brief but illuminating section on the Our Father, also known as the "Lord's Prayer" because the Lord himself taught it.

The Our Father is found in both Luke's and Matthew's Gospels. In Matthew, it is part of the Sermon on the Mount (chapters 5–7), where Jesus also gave us the Beatitudes. The Our Father embodies the Beatitudes, which St. John Paul II and Pope Benedict saw as the "self-portrait of Christ" and the blueprint for holiness (*Veritatis Splendor*, 16; cf. Angelus, November 1, 2008).

From the earliest times, the Our Father was "handed on" to those who were baptized. Reborn in Christ as members of the Church, we become capable of "speaking to God with the very word of God" (CCC, 2769). The true home of the Our Father is in the celebration of the Eucharist, which embodies its seven petitions (*Compendium*, 581).

In the Our Father, we approach God the Father with simplicity and trust. When the eternal Son became man, he revealed the Father to us. The Holy Spirit joins us to Christ so that we may have knowledge of the Father and become his children. As we call upon God as our Father, the Spirit rekindles our desire to live as his sons and daughters (*Compendium*, 582–583).

Centered on God

Every word counts in the Our Father, beginning with the simple word "our." To call God "our" Father is to affirm our relationship with him. In saying "our" Father, we also say that the Church of Christ is the communion of those who call God their Father (*Compendium*, 584). Thus, the Our Father is implicitly a prayer for the unity of the Church and the unity of the entire human family (585).

In adding the phrase "who art in heaven," we acknowledge the utter grandeur of God, who is not diminished or "domesticated" when we call him our "Father." Rather, in Christ and the Holy Spirit, we are lifted up to share the Father's glory (*Compendium*, 586).

After these opening words come the seven petitions. The first three praise God for his glory even as we ask to be drawn ever more deeply into that glory. The last four ask God to bend down to assist us in our need: "to feed us, to forgive us, to sustain us in temptations, and to free us from the Evil One" (*Compendium*, 587).

With the first petition—"Hallowed be thy Name"—we are asking to be made holy by professing God's name and by making it known to the ends of the earth (*Compendium*, 588–589).

In the second petition—"Thy Kingdom come"—we pray for Christ to come in glory at the end of time and also ask to share in the holiness of the kingdom of God (*Compendium*, 590). In effect, we are asking to be equipped to build a "civilization of love."

The third petition—"Thy will be done on earth as it is in heaven"—involves praying for a share in the perfect and loving obedience of Christ. We ask the Father to unite our will with that of his Son, just as he has done in the life of the Blessed Virgin Mary and all the saints. We also beg that God's plan of salvation be realized in our lives and that we may know and do his will (*Compendium*, 591).

Praying for Our Needs

The final four petitions relate to our human condition and begin with a prayer for "our daily bread." Here we ask God for what we need while recognizing that we do not live on "bread alone, / but by every word that comes forth from the mouth of God" (Matthew 4:4; cf. Deuteronomy 8:3). Thus, we seek to be nourished by the living word of God and by the Body of Christ in the Eucharist (*Compendium*, 592–593).

In the fifth petition—"Forgive us our trespasses as we forgive those who trespass against us"—we beg God to forgive our sins, confident as we are in the power of his love. As we say these words, however, we can hear Jesus saying to us, "Blessed are the merciful, / for they will be shown mercy" (Matthew 5:7). Even God's mercy cannot enter a heart that is hardened by hatred. In opening our hearts to Christ's love, we find the grace to forgive our enemies. When we do so, we share in divine mercy and the peace of God's kingdom (*Compendium*, 594–595).

By the sixth petition—"Lead us not into temptation"—we ask God to stand by us so that we may clearly know right from wrong, have the strength to persevere in holiness, and be one with Jesus who overcame temptation by prayer (*Compendium*, 596).

In the final petition, we pray, "Deliver us from evil." Here we ask to be delivered from the grasp of Satan who works to harm us both physically and spiritually. We make this prayer not only for ourselves, but indeed for all the Church and for the world. We pray with confidence because we believe that Christ has already conquered sin and death by his own death and resurrection (*Compendium*, 597).

The last word of the Our Father is "Amen," by which we express our assent to the prayer Jesus taught us. May our lives also express our assent to this prayer, which is itself a compendium of the Christian faith.

For Personal Reflection and Group Discussion

1. Have you ever thought of the Lord's Prayer as "speaking to God with the very word of God"? How might a constant awareness of this truth help you when you pray it?

_____

_____

_____

_____

_____

2. Do you find it difficult to call God "Father"? Why or why not? What does it mean to you personally that you are a son or daughter of God?

_____

_____

_____

_____

_____

3. Do you consciously pray to have a share in Christ's loving obedience to the Father? Is there a situation in your life now where this might apply?

_____

_____

_____

_____

_____

4. Do you have any reservation or difficulty about praying the petition "Forgive us our trespasses as we forgive those who trespass against us"? Ask the Holy Spirit for grace and help if you need to extend forgiveness to anyone or repair a broken relationship in order to freely and genuinely offer this prayer.

_____

_____

_____

_____

_____

5. Recall and share about a few instances when praying the Our Father was especially significant and meaningful to you.

_____

_____

_____

_____

_____

Conclusion: The Truth Is Symphonic

THE "FOUR PILLARS" OF FAITH PRESENTED IN THE CATECHISM ARE INTERCONNECTED PARTS OF A WHOLE

At the conclusion of our study of the *Compendium*, let us examine again the purpose of this book. Simply put, it aims to help Catholics grow in understanding of the faith and engage in the new evangelization. After all, a genuine understanding of the Church's faith enables us to read Scripture with greater insight and to share more deeply in the Mass and the sacraments. It helps us live according to the gospel and guides us in the ways of prayer.

By knowing, loving, and living the faith, we are better prepared to invite others to return home to Christ and the Church and are better able to attract those searching for the fullness of truth. We thereby impact individual lives and build up the Church as the body of Christ, transforming our culture from within. As Pope Francis wrote in his apostolic exhortation *Evangelii Gaudium*, Christians "should appear as people who wish to share their joy, who point to a horizon of beauty and who invite others to a delicious banquet. It is not by proselytizing that the Church grows, but 'by attraction'" (14).

Yet all these goals will elude us unless we step back to look at the faith, not just in its component parts, but as a whole.

The Mystery of Faith

If our faith were simply a long checklist of unrelated items to be believed and acted upon, then it would be burdensome. As it is, far too many people see the faith in this way. But by presenting the "four pillars" of the faith, the *Catechism of the Catholic Church* and its *Compendium* show us how all aspects of the Church's faith are interrelated in truth and beauty.

What we believe (the Profession of the Christian Faith) gives rise to how we worship as a Church (the Celebration of the Christian Mystery) and to how we live (Life in Christ) and pray (Christian Prayer).

Far more than an onerous checklist, Christianity is a way of life. It sheds the light and beauty of God's truth on why we were created, who we are, how we should live, and what our ultimate destiny is. As the Second Vatican Council said so profoundly, "The truth is that only in the mystery of the incarnate Word does the mystery of man take on light" (*Gaudium et Spes*, 22).

To clarify this point, I would like to borrow an idea from the title of a book by the late Swiss theologian Hans Urs von Balthasar, *Truth Is Symphonic*. The Church's faith might be compared with a beautiful symphony. Often, each movement of a symphony has a leitmotif, a fundamental musical theme that recurs with variations. Sometimes the theme is played softly, sometimes dramatically, sometimes jarringly, but the ears of an attentive and informed listener can pick up the theme, absorb it, participate in it, and come away with a unified sense of the genius of the composer and his composition.

The fundamental theme, or leitmotif, of the Church's faith is what St. Paul refers to as "the mystery" (1 Timothy 3:16)—the plan of creation and redemption that the Triune God, shrouded in glory, set into motion. God is love, and he created the world so that human beings, created in his image and likeness, could enter into a communion of love with him. However, after we had estranged ourselves from him and from one another through sin, God revealed himself to the chosen people. From this people, he chose Mary, who became the earthly mother of God's divine Son.

God's Plan and Our Response

By his preaching and miracles, and ultimately by giving his life for us and in rising triumphant from the dead, Jesus revealed that the Father's love, for which we were created, is stronger than sin and death. Jesus established the Church so that in the power of the Holy Spirit, we could share in his redeeming love until the end of time.

This mystery is God's masterpiece in which the great themes of creation and redemption sound in harmony. Here the love of an eternal God and the meaning of human history are given voice. As this mystery unfolds in human history, it is full of drama and diversity and rife with the discordant notes of human infidelity. But the love of God always prevails.

By catching sight of God's plan of creation and redemption, we also see how Scripture and Sacred Tradition speak in human terms with one divine voice. We see the unity of Scripture itself, and we grasp how both faith and reason lift up the human spirit. So too, we perceive how our worship in the Mass and the sacraments is like a counterpoint, a graced response to the gift of God's love.

In the same way, Christian morality is not merely a jumble of rules like random notes on a musical score but is rather the coherent way in which the theme of Christ's goodness and love is to resonate in our intentions, decisions, and actions. Finally, in Christian prayer we are given the grace to respond, intimately and personally, to Christ's love echoing in the depths of our being.

The faith of the Church is indeed unified, true, beautiful, good, and life-giving. Let us stand united in love in proclaiming and living the faith for the glory of God, for the salvation of our souls, and for the good of the Church and the world.

For Personal Reflection and Group Discussion

1. Why does a better understanding of our faith help us to become better evangelists? What have you learned that will help you in this regard?

_____

_____

_____

_____

_____

2. Have you ever been tempted to view Christianity as a set of rules rather than a way of life? How does friendship with Jesus change the way we look at our faith?

_____

_____

_____

_____

_____

3. What is one thing you have learned from this study that changes the way you view God and his Church? The way you pray and worship?

_____

_____

_____

_____

_____

4. Why is it important to look at our faith as a unified whole rather than as disparate parts? What is the backdrop behind the story of God's creation and redemption?

_____

_____

_____

_____

_____

5. How will you live and proclaim your faith in a way that gives glory to God? Think of one or two things that you can do to concretely express your decision to live your life for Christ.

_____

_____

_____

_____

_____

the WORD
among us ®
The *Spirit* of Catholic Living

T his book was published by The Word Among Us. Since 1981, The
Word Among Us has been answering the call of the Second Vatican
Council to help Catholic laypeople encounter Christ in the Scriptures.

The name of our company comes from the prologue to the Gospel
of John and reflects the vision and purpose of all of our publications:
to be an instrument of the Spirit, whose desire is to manifest Jesus'
presence in and to the children of God. In this way, we hope to contribute to the Church's ongoing mission of proclaiming the gospel
to the world so that all people would know the love and mercy of
our Lord and grow ever more deeply in love with him.

Our monthly devotional magazine, *The Word Among Us*, features
meditations on the daily and Sunday Mass readings, and currently
reaches more than one million Catholics in North America and
another half million Catholics in one hundred countries around the
world. Our book division, The Word Among Us Press, publishes
numerous books, Bible studies, and pamphlets that help Catholics
grow in their faith.

To learn more about who we are and what we publish, log on to
our website at www.wau.org. There you will find a variety of Catholic resources that will help you grow in your faith.

Embrace His Word, Listen to God . . .

wau.org